To Bill and Mary.

hope you will enjoy the recipes and the read

with best Wishes.

*[signature]*

Happy cooking

Joyeux Noël

The Vineyard    25·12·11

# DANIEL GALMICHE

# *FRENCH* BRASSERIE *COOKBOOK*

## THE HEART OF FRENCH HOME COOKING

DUNCAN BAIRD PUBLISHERS

LONDON

# FRENCH BRASSERIE COOKBOOK

Daniel Galmiche

First published in the United Kingdom and Ireland
in 2011 by
Duncan Baird Publishers Ltd
Sixth Floor, Castle House
75–76 Wells Street
London W1T 3QH

Conceived, created and designed by
Duncan Baird Publishers

**Managing Editor:** Grace Cheetham
**Editors:** Camilla Davis and Nicole Bator
**French Consultant:** Séverine Jeauneau
**Managing Designer:** Manisha Patel
**Production:** Uzma Taj
**Commissioned Photography:** Yuki Sugiura
**Photography Assistant:** Mick English
**Food Stylists:** Daniel Galmiche with Aya Nishimura
**Prop Stylist:** Wei Tang

British Library Cataloguing-in-Publication Data:
A CIP record for this book is available from the
British Library

ISBN: 978-1-84483-992-6

10 9 8 7 6 5 4 3 2 1

Typeset in ITC New Baskerville and MetaPlus
Colour reproduction by Colourscan, Singapore
Printed in China by Imago

**PUBLISHER'S NOTE**
While every care has been taken in compiling the recipes
for this book, Duncan Baird Publishers, or any other
persons who have been involved in working on this
publication, cannot accept responsibility for any errors
or omissions, inadvertent or not, that may be found in
the recipes or text, nor for any problems that may arise
as a result of preparing one of these recipes. If you are
pregnant or breastfeeding or have any special dietary
requirements or medical conditions, it is advisable
to consult a medical professional before following
any of the recipes contained in this book. Some wild
mushrooms can be fatally poisonous, however you cook
them. Neither the publisher nor the author can take
any responsibility for any illness or other unintended
consequences resulting from following any of the advice
or suggestions in this book.

**NOTES ON THE RECIPES**
Unless otherwise stated:
All recipes serve 4
Use medium eggs, fruit and vegetables
Use fresh ingredients, including herbs and chillies
Do not mix metric and imperial measurements
1 tsp = 5ml  1 tbsp = 15ml  1 cup = 250ml

# *Dedication*

To five very special people: to my mum, Anne-Marie, and my late Great-Aunt Suzanne for their love and passion for cooking, which they passed on to me; to my first teacher, the late Yves Lalloz, who took me on when I was 15 and guided me wisely through my three-year apprenticeship with him; and finally to my wife, Claire, for her charm, friendship and unconditional support, and my son, Antoine, whose love of life and food is contagious. My profound thanks to you all.

# FOREWORD

Ever since my first wonderful meal at Harvey's in Bristol many years ago, I have been a great fan of Daniel's cooking. He is a true master of contemporary French cuisine and his passion, expertise and attention to detail have ensured that dining at his table is never a disappointment. Who better, then, to teach the classics of the French kitchen?

The *French Brasserie Cookbook* contains all the recipes that you would expect, from Cheese Soufflé to Duck Rillettes, from Bouillabaisse to the perfect tarte tatin, but many of the classics have been given Daniel's unique twists. Alongside traditional onion soup, cassoulet and Beef Bourguignon are Lime Risotto, Moules Marinières with Lemongrass & Chilli, and Coffee Crème Caramel. It's a fantastic combination of recipes and flavours.

And despite Daniel's huge talent as a Michelin-starred chef, this book is extremely accessible. It is practical, unfussy and easy to use but, most satisfyingly, it is full of inspiring recipes that will immediately transport you to a French brasserie in your own home.

*Heston Blumenthal*

# Contents

# INTRODUCTION

### *What is it about brasseries?*

I'm sitting on my balcony at home, musing on food as usual and asking myself what it is about brasseries that we all love so much. So I'm thinking ... you take a trip to Paris for a weekend and find yourself wandering happily through the wide boulevards, cobbled side streets and paved courtyards. You spot a stylish yet unassuming terrace and think you might sit outside and watch the world go by for an hour or so – but something draws you in. Is it the warm ambience and friendly faces? Is it the dark polished wood of the bar and ornate handles of the bar dispenser ready to serve you beer on tap? Is it the shining brass, the comfortable banquettes or the stunning art deco mirrors? Or is it quite simply the fantastic and mouth-watering smell of food drifting out of the kitchen? Whatever it is, it's irresistible.

As soon as you enter a brasserie in France, you are struck by a feeling of timelessness. You're ushered to a table by a *garçon de café* with a long, white apron, black bow tie and a quirky sense of humour. He seems to glide effortlessly amid the hustle and bustle of the busy interior and settles you into a cosy corner made more intimate by the stained-glass partition that boasts an elaborate hand-painted scene in the style of Toulouse Lautrec or a simple *fleur de lys*. You gaze around at the tarnished candlesticks and glamorous chandeliers and yet there is nothing grand or intimidating about being here – there's too much laughter and conviviality in the air for that. And it occurs to you that brasseries are something of a paradox: sophisticated yet informal, chic yet unpretentious, boisterous yet elegant.

Popular for more than a century, brasseries are the fabled haunt of artists and writers, the meeting place of politicians and prime ministers, an attraction where both tourists and locals alike linger to see and be seen. But it's not for the fashion or the frivolity that they gather here – it's for the food.

## So how did it all start?

The word 'brasserie' actually means 'brewery' in French. In 1864, Frédéric Bofinger, a brewer from Alsace in northeastern France (the region that borders my own, Franche-Comté), made his way to Paris and opened a tiny bar in the heart of the Marais and Faubourg Saint-Antoine area. It served little more than draft beer and sauerkraut. At that time, numerous people were moving to Paris from war-torn Alsace in search of work, so there was a ready market. Beer on tap was unheard of in Paris back then and the quality of the sauerkraut was second to none. The combination took the city by storm and in no time brasseries were springing up all over Paris. The rest of France soon followed, and I think, for this reason, Bofinger could rightly claim to be the father of the Parisian brasserie. What started as a smoky bar filled with Alsatian refugees grew into a magnificent dining room with polished wood, gleaming brass and a stained-glass dome.

Today, brasseries are fashionable hotspots where politicians continue to rub shoulders with artists – but there is more to them than glamour. Brasseries are popular because the food they serve is homely, heart-warming and delicious. You can eat a simple sandwich or enjoy a *grand repas*, and they will often serve everything from early breakfasts right through to late suppers in the small hours. Among the famous brasseries in Paris are: Bofinger, La Coupole and Brasserie Lipp, to name but a few. However, no matter where you are in France, if you find a good brasserie, you will find a good meal – and you won't have to pay a fortune for it either.

Some brasseries will be modern and chic and some laden with so much history they are practically national monuments. But choose carefully – there are plenty on main streets, but the best ones are often tucked away down side streets and hidden behind porchways.

How many restaurants can boast the illustrious likes of Ernest Hemingway, F. Scott Fitzgerald, Salvador Dalí, Henry

Miller, Pablo Picasso and Henri Matisse among their clientele? Well, La Coupole can. Few people take a trip to Paris without visiting this renowned brasserie at least once.

It is said that, in 1944, when the Allied armies were poised to move into Paris to liberate it, the writer Ernest Hemingway became frustrated at the delay because he wanted to eat at his favourite brasserie. Borrowing a car, he drove unprotected into the French capital a whole day before the official liberators made their move and decided to 'liberate' La Coupole personally. The things we will do for the love of food!

### From region to region

Brasseries make the most of local produce. There is a kind of regional pride, which ensures that you will always be served the best of whatever is grown or produced in the region. So eating in a brasserie in the South of France is a very different experience to eating in one in, say, Brittany. They all promote their own regional classics, often alongside well-known dishes from other areas. In Franche-Comté (my region), it could be Morteau sausage with sautéed potatoes and melted Vacherin Mont d'Or cheese. Up the road in Alsace, it could be *choucroute* (sauerkraut) or *baeckeoffe* (a kind of hotpot of potatoes, onion and pork). In Brest in Brittany, it could be seabass baked in a sea-salt crust, and in Paris it might be coq au vin. And if you are in one of France's great brasseries, you will probably find all these specialities on one menu. Whatever region you find yourself in, brasseries will always offer a great variety of food. So whether you want to have a quick meeting over a coffee and a croissant or to while away the hours with a friend over steak frites and a glass of red wine, you're in the right place.

### Home from home

Actually, cooking French food doesn't need to be complicated, and bringing brasserie dishes into the home is returning them to their rightful place. After all, this is where most of them started, as most popular regional dishes served in brasseries would have been the ones that were originally firm family favourites. For example, if you lived in Nancy in Lorraine, you would probably have eaten quiche lorraine; and if you lived in Bouches-du-Rhône, near Marseilles, it would have been bouillabaisse (a fish dish made with saffron and tomatoes), *boudin noir* (black pudding), coq au vin, *tarte aux pommes* (apple tart), crème caramel – all dishes that were cooked at home long before they were available in brasseries. Perhaps that's the reason why they have a special place in our hearts.

The love of food has been with me as long as I can remember. My experience has come from sources that range from my grandmother to Michel Roux, but for me, the journey started with the wonderful home cooking of my grandmother. (I call her Grand-Mère in this book, although she was actually my great aunt; she took my natural grandmother's place so readily after her passing that it would have felt odd for us children to call her anything else.) My first memory is of Grand-Mère's kitchen on the farm my grandparents owned in Franche-Comté, where I passed much of my childhood. I spent most Sunday afternoons and a large part of the summer holidays playing in haystacks around the farm with my brother and sister. If we weren't chasing cows, we were stealing cherries from the neighbouring farm, stuffing as many as we could into our mouths and pockets before the farmer could catch us. Even now when I walk through fields, I find it hard to resist such temptations – old habits die hard, I guess!

If I close my eyes and think back, I can still recall the scent of freshly baked cakes luring me in from the fields. It wasn't long before I was in that kitchen constantly: watching, learning, helping Grand-Mère prepare the fruit I'd collected. I'm told that, at the age of five, I stood in the middle of the kitchen and announced, 'When I grow up, I'm going to be a chef!' Funny how history has a habit of repeating itself: I have a beautiful son who, strangely enough, at the age of five, stood in the middle of my kitchen and said, 'When I grow up, I'm going to be a chef!' Well, what can you do?

My father, who was also called Daniel, played a large part, too. He was very close to nature, and walks were a daily routine that he always said he couldn't do without. There was nothing he loved more – apart, perhaps, from hunting for food and then sharing the meal with family and friends. My father was what we call in France *une fine gueule*, which I can only translate as 'somebody who really loves good food'. We used to walk through the ancient, plentiful forests and he would tell me about the plants, the trees and the animal footprints that we came across. I hold such special memories of these days.

Papa and I usually went pheasant hunting on a Saturday and so would be woken up on Sunday morning by the scent of delicately smoked bacon and pheasant roasting in red wine, which Maman (the other wonderful cook of my childhood) had been preparing since who knows what time. Sometimes there would even be an apple tart in the oven at the same time and the combination of aromas would drift up the stairs and pull us out of our cosy beds. The pheasant was normally prepared with braised cabbage and roasted turnips glazed in the pheasant *jus*. Utterly delicious and quintessential French home cooking.

Maman was another great cook taught by Grand-Mère (she had no choice but to be a great cook because Papa loved food so much). I just happened to be around when she was cooking – eating, tasting and cooking – completely unaware that my future was being shaped at that time.

When I became an apprentice chef at the age of fifteen, I had no idea how hard it was going to be. I had to complete three years before I could reach the next stage of becoming a commis chef, and there was still a long road ahead. I was catapulted from restaurant to restaurant, learning more and more as I went until, finally, I was given my first Head Chef position. Having reached this position, it started all over again. Passion, hard work and sheer bullheadedness somehow got me where I am today.

I hope my love of simple brasserie food not only encourages you to cook at home and enjoy the food you would normally just eat on holiday, but also inspires you to become hunters and gatherers again. How much more fun is it to take the children fruit picking or fishing than to drag them round the supermarket on a Saturday afternoon? I'm not expecting anyone to go out and spear the nearest wild boar, just to entice you to go, say, strawberry picking or foraging for wild garlic.

In this book, you will find some lovely, uncomplicated dishes that come from all over France. Some are traditional with a twist (for example, I have made them lighter or more up-to-date); others are specialities from particular regions but made my way. All of these recipes are ones that I cook at home with my wife, Claire, and son, Antoine. Hopefully, once you've tried them, you will make them again and again. I wanted to create a book that's not too 'cheffy' (the kind that only chefs can follow), a straightforward home cookbook that's fun to read and inspires you to cook some really terrific French food – so don't leave it on the coffee table! If you use this cookbook on a regular basis, it will make me very happy.

## A few technical terms

Here is a glossary of some of the culinary terms and techniques I've used when writing these recipes – you may be familiar with some of them but less so others.

**TO JULIENNE:** Cut vegetables or fruit zest into thin sticks 1–2mm/$\frac{1}{32}$–$\frac{1}{16}$in thick and 3cm/1$\frac{1}{4}$in long, using a knife or a mandoline. They are generally cooked in butter (and the zest in syrup), covered, until quite soft. Raw vegetables that are to be served as an hors d'oeuvre can also be cut in juliennes.

**TO BOIL:** When using a deep saucepan with the amount of liquid required, you bring it to the boil over direct heat and maintain it for the specific time given in your recipe method.

**TO POACH:** When you cook food in a liquid (this can be water, bouillon, stock, or syrup) that is very hot but not bubbling, at a temperature just below the simmer. Suitable for gently cooking poultry, meat, vegetables, eggs or fruit, and delicate foods that could break in a vigorously bubbling liquid.

**TO SIMMER:** When you cook food in a hot liquid kept just below the boiling point and bubbling very gently.

**TO BRAISE:** When you roast or brown a piece of meat, poultry or vegetable in fat, then add a small amount of liquid and simmer in a covered pot over a low heat.

**TO FRY:** To cook in hot fat (oil, butter or lard), with food either totally submerged (deep frying) or fat coming halfway up the food (pan-frying). Often used to cook vegetable juliennes, potatoes, fish and chicken.

**TO GRIDDLE:** When you chargrill meat, poultry, fish or vegetables in a heavy-based frying pan over a high heat. There are two types of griddle pans – ridged and flat. For my recipes I use the ridged variety that produces charred lines. These look impressive and create a lovely, gentle, caramelized flavour.

**TO SAUTÉ:** When you put a little fat (oil, butter or lard) in a shallow pan, add potatoes, vegetables, mushrooms, meat, poultry or fruits, and quickly toss them over a medium to high heat to brown or cook through. It is important to keep the food moving around the pan.

**TO DEGLAZE:** When, after sautéeing, you add a liquid, such as alcohol, juice or vinegar, stir to dissolve the caramelized brown bits in the pan, and then allow half to evaporate quickly. If you are using alcohol, you can set it alight (*flamber* it).

**TO REDUCE:** When you have a lot of liquid in a pan, and you need to decrease the volume over a medium to high heat. Make sure you get to the level or consistency directed in the recipe method.

**CONFIT:** When a piece of pork, goose, duck or turkey is cooked in its own fat and stored in a pot, it is called *confit*. A vegetable confit would be done in olive oil. To 'confit' something is one of the oldest means of storing food.

**RAGOÛT:** A stew made from meat, poultry, game, fish or vegetables that are cut into pieces of uniform size and shape and cooked with or without first being browned in a sauté pan. It is generally flavoured with herbs and spices. The ragoût dates back to the 17th century when, in classic French, the word was used to describe anything that stimulated the appetite.

**TIAN:** The name given to a dish that consists of alternate layers of sliced vegetables. It may be made with or without onions and garlic, but would definitely be sprinkled with herbs and well seasoned. It is also the name of Provençal earthenware pots.

*Mayonnaise au safran*

*Pâte à tarte Grand-Mère*

*Fond d'agneau*

*Vinaigrette*

*Pâte brisée*

*Crème pâtissière*

*Pâte sucrée*

*Pâte à choux*

*Pâte à crêpes*

## Les Bases
# THE BASICS

Stocks, sauces and pastry are essential ingredients in many classic French dishes, and in this chapter I will be showing you how to make them. With my stocks, I like to have the real flavour of the main ingredient coming through – the intensity is the vital thing. Sauces are important too. Although they are often made with a few, simple ingredients, they can transform a plain dish into something really special. I'm passionate about good pastry, which is the foundation of many of my favourite recipes and essential to a good pie or tart – whether it is savoury or sweet.

## *Fond de volaille*

# CHICKEN STOCK

*Makes 2l/70fl oz/8 cups*
*Preparation time 10 minutes, plus*
*1 hour cooling*
*Cooking time 2 hours 40 minutes*

2kg/4lb 8oz chicken wings or bones,
or 2 chicken carcasses

1 thyme sprig

2 carrots, peeled and halved
lengthways

1 small handful of curly parsley
stems

1 small onion, unpeeled and halved

6 black peppercorns

Put all the ingredients in a large, heavy-based saucepan, cover with 4l/140fl oz/16 cups cold water and bring to the boil over a high heat. As soon as the stock starts to boil, foam will begin to form on the surface. Reduce the heat to low and skim off the foam, using a ladle, then simmer gently, uncovered, for 2–2½ hours. By this time the liquid will have reduced by half and the flavour will have intensified. Remove from the heat, pass the stock through a sieve, using a ladle to help you, then leave it to cool for at least 1 hour. Your stock is then ready to use.

If you want to freeze your stock, divide the cooled stock into small plastic tubs with lids, leaving some space for it to expand, and pop the containers in the freezer. Your stock will keep for up to 4 weeks.

## *Fond d'agneau*

# LAMB STOCK

*Makes 2l/70fl oz/8 cups*
*Preparation time 15 minutes, plus*
*1 hour cooling*
*Cooking time 3 hours 50 minutes*

1.25kg/2lb 12oz lamb bones,
trimmed and prepared by your
butcher

2 tbsp olive oil

1 rosemary or thyme sprig

2 parsley sprigs

1 garlic bulb, unpeeled and halved
crossways

1 small onion, unpeeled and
quartered

6 black peppercorns

2 large tomatoes, quartered

Preheat the oven to 180°C/350°F/gas 4. Put the bones in a baking tray and roast for 20 minutes or until golden brown, stirring occasionally to make sure they colour evenly. Remove the bones from the tray and put them in a large, heavy-based saucepan. Add all the remaining ingredients, except the tomatoes, and cook over a medium heat for 10 minutes. Add the tomatoes, then cook for a further 10 minutes.

Add 4l/140fl oz/16 cups cold water and bring to the boil over a high heat. As soon as the stock starts to boil, foam will begin to form on the surface. Reduce the heat to low and skim off the foam, using a ladle. Simmer for 1 hour, uncovered, then top up the water to its previous level and simmer for a further 2 hours. By this time the liquid will have reduced by half. Remove from the heat, pass the stock through a sieve, using a ladle to help you, then leave it to cool for at least 1 hour. It should be a lovely, shiny, clear, golden brown colour. Your stock is then ready to use.

If you want to freeze your stock, divide the cooled stock into small plastic tubs with lids, leaving some space for it to expand, and pop the containers in the freezer. Your stock will keep for up to 4 weeks.

## *Fumet de poisson*

# FISH STOCK

*Makes 2l/70fl oz/8 cups*
*Preparation time 10 minutes, plus*
*  1 hour cooling*
*Cooking time 2 hours 40 minutes*

1.25kg/2lb 12oz fresh fish bones, flesh removed

1 small handful of curly parsley stems

1 small onion, unpeeled and quartered

1 thyme sprig

1 celery stick, peeled and halved

6 black peppercorns

Place the fish bones in a large bowl, cover with cold water and rest for 10 minutes, then rinse thoroughly using a sieve. Repeat three times.

Put the bones in a large heavy-based saucepan with all the other ingredients, cover with 4l/140fl oz/16 cups cold water and bring to the boil over a high heat. As soon as the stock starts to boil, foam will begin to form on the surface. Reduce the heat to low and skim off the foam, using a ladle, then simmer gently, uncovered, for 2–2$^1$/2 hours. By this time the liquid will have reduced by half and the flavour will have intensified. Remove from the heat, pass the stock through a sieve, using a ladle to help you, then leave it to cool for at least 1 hour. Your stock is then ready to use.

If you want to freeze your stock, divide the cooled stock into small plastic tubs with lids, leaving some space for it to expand, and pop the containers in the freezer. Your stock will keep for up to 4 weeks.

---

## *Bouillon de légumes*

# VEGETABLE STOCK

*Makes 1.5l/52fl oz/6 cups*
*Preparation time 15 minutes, plus*
*  1 hour cooling*
*Cooking time 2 hours 15 minutes*

2 tbsp olive oil

1 celery stick, peeled and chopped, or 1 small handful of celery leaves

1 thyme sprig

1 spring onion, chopped

1 handful of parsley stems, chopped

1 garlic clove

2 carrots, peeled and halved lengthways

2 new potatoes, halved

6 black peppercorns

2 button mushrooms, halved

Briefly warm the oil in a large saucepan over a medium heat. Add all the remaining ingredients and cook, partially covered, for 10 minutes. Add 3l/105fl oz/12 cups cold water and bring to the boil over a high heat, then reduce the heat to low and simmer, uncovered, for 2 hours or until reduced by half. Remove from the heat, pass the stock through a sieve, using a ladle to help you, then leave it to cool for at least 1 hour. Your stock is then ready to use.

If you want to freeze your stock, divide the cooled stock into small plastic tubs with lids, leaving some space for it to expand, and pop the containers in the freezer. Your stock will keep for up to 4 weeks.

## *Vinaigrette*

# FRENCH VINAIGRETTE

*Makes 185ml/6fl oz/¾ cup*
*Preparation time 5 minutes*

2 tsp Dijon mustard

2 tbsp red or white wine vinegar or
  balsamic vinegar

125ml/4fl oz/½ cup olive oil or
  rapeseed oil

sea salt and freshly ground black
  pepper

In a small bowl or jug, whisk together the mustard, vinegar and
2 tablespoons water, then whisk in the oil. You should have quite
a thick, glossy liquid. Season with salt and pepper.

Use straightaway or cover and keep in the fridge for up to 1 week.

## *Sauce hollandaise*

# HOLLANDAISE SAUCE

*Makes 425ml/15fl oz/1¾ cups*
*Preparation time 5 minutes*
*Cooking time 25 minutes*

2 tbsp white wine vinegar

2 large egg yolks, beaten

350g/12oz butter, melted

juice of ½ lemon

sea salt and freshly ground black
  pepper

Put 6 tablespoons water in a small saucepan over a medium heat. Add
the vinegar, season with salt and pepper and simmer for 2 minutes until
reduced by half and the liquid becomes syrupy. Transfer the vinegar
reduction to a heatproof bowl and rest it over a saucepan of gently
simmering water, making sure the bottom of the bowl does not touch the
water (this is called a bain-marie). Add the egg yolks and beat the mixture
continuously over a low heat until it turns white, thickens and the liquid
coats the back of a spoon. Don't let the water boil or your sauce will turn
into scrambled eggs!

Now add the melted butter to the vinegar reduction a little at a time,
omitting any 'milk solids' that form at the bottom of the pan, whisking
continuously. When it starts to thicken, add 1 tablespoon water, then
continue adding the butter until it is all incorporated. The mixture should be
smooth and light – you may need to add a little more water to achieve this
consistency. Season again with salt and pepper and keep warm in the bain-
marie until ready to serve. Just before serving, squeeze in a few drops of
lemon juice. Taste and add more juice if you like a stronger lemony flavour.

*Mayonnaise au safran*

# SAFFRON MAYONNAISE

*Makes 200ml/7fl oz/scant 1 cup*
*Preparation time 10 minutes*
*Cooking time 5 minutes*

a good pinch of saffron threads

2 egg yolks

1 tbsp French mustard

150ml/5fl oz/scant ⅔ cup
  sunflower or grapeseed oil

1 garlic clove, finely chopped

a squeeze of lemon juice (optional)

sea salt and freshly ground black
  pepper

To create your essence of saffron, put the saffron and 2 tablespoons water in a small saucepan over a low heat. Simmer for 4–5 minutes to allow the saffron to release its flavour and colour. When it is a strong deep-orange colour, strain the liquid into a bowl and, using a whisk, beat the egg yolks and mustard into it. Season with salt and pepper and a few drops of lemon, if liked, then drizzle in the oil, a little at a time, stirring continuously. Add the garlic and then whisk in 2 tablespoons hot water to help it bind. The mayonnaise should be glossy and luscious!

Keep in the fridge and serve cold.

*Sauce vierge*

# SAUCE VIERGE

*Makes 150ml/5fl oz/scant ⅔ cup*
*Preparation time 10 minutes*
*Cooking time 3 minutes*

4 tbsp extra virgin olive oil

1 shallot, chopped

1 tomato, deseeded and diced

juice of ½ lime

1 tbsp balsamic vinegar

1 handful of flat-leaf parsley, finely
  chopped

sea salt and freshly ground black
  pepper

Put the oil in a small saucepan and briefly warm it over a low heat for about 30 seconds. Add the shallot and cook for 2 minutes. Remove from the heat and stir in the tomato, lime juice and balsamic vinegar. Just before serving, add the parsley and season with salt and pepper. Enjoy warm drizzled over your dish.

Baking was Grand-Mère Suzanne's thing, and most of the time, she did it without measuring. She knew whether something was right just by looking at it, and when it came to cakes and tarts, no one could match her. Grand-Mère's pastry is sweet, and is great for apple, pear and mixed-fruit tarts – actually it's great for all desserts in general.

*Pâte à tarte de Grand-Mère*

# GRAND-MÈRE'S SWEET PASTRY

*Makes enough for a 28cm/11¼in tin*
*Preparation time 15 minutes, plus*
*30 minutes chilling*

125g/4½oz unsalted butter, roughly diced and softened to room temperature

85g/3oz/⅔ cup icing sugar, sifted, plus extra for dusting

1 egg

2 egg yolks

250g/9oz/2 cups plain flour, plus extra for kneading the dough

Put the butter and sugar in a large mixing bowl and beat with a wooden spoon until nice and creamy. Stir in the egg and egg yolks, then add the flour and mix everything together with your fingers until it forms a lovely crumbly texture. Press the mixture together to form a ball. On a lightly-floured surface, knead the pastry with the palm of your hand for 1–2 minutes, or until it forms a ball easily and is soft to the touch. Watch out – don't overwork the pastry or it will go back to the crumbly texture! Flatten it slightly with the palm of your hand, wrap it in cling film and leave in the fridge for at least 30 minutes before use – this helps it to relax – and, meanwhile, so can you!

*Pâte sucrée*

# SWEET SHORT PASTRY

*Makes enough for a 28cm/11¼in tin*
*Preparation time 15 minutes, plus*
*2 hours chilling*

175g/6oz butter, softened

a pinch of salt

1 tsp caster sugar

1 egg yolk

3 tbsp milk or water, at room temperature

250g/9oz/2 cups plain flour

Put the butter, salt, sugar, egg yolk and milk in a mixing bowl and mix together by hand. Add the flour slowly, mixing until just combined. Be careful not to overwork it or it will become too elastic. When the pastry is ready, either wrap it in a clean cotton tea towel or put it on a plate, covered with a clean cotton tea towel, and leave in the fridge for 2 hours before using – this will relax the dough and make it easier to use.

## *Pâte brisée*
# SAVOURY SHORT PASTRY

*Makes enough for a 28cm/11¼in tin*
*Preparation time 15 minutes, plus*
*2 hours chilling*

125g/4½oz butter, roughly
diced and softened to room
temperature

250g/9oz/2 cups plain flour, plus
extra for kneading the dough

a pinch of salt

1 egg yolk

3 tbsp milk or water

Put the butter, flour and salt in a mixing bowl and mix together by hand until it is a crumbly, powdery texture. Add the egg yolk and milk and continue working the pastry until the ingredients are combined and the texture is smooth. On a lightly floured surface, knead the pastry for about 1–2 minutes until silky smooth. When the pastry is ready, either wrap it in a clean cotton tea towel or put it on a plate, covered with a clean cotton tea towel and leave in the fridge for 2 hours before using – this will relax the dough and make it easier to use.

## *Pâte à choux*
# CHOUX PASTRY

*Makes 30–40 profiteroles*
*Preparation time 15 minutes, plus*
*40 minutes resting and making the*
*crème pâtissière*
*Cooking time 40 minutes*

180g/6¼oz butter

5g/⅛oz/scant 1 tsp salt

scant 1 tbsp sugar

250g/9oz/2 cups plain flour

8 small eggs

a few drops of vanilla extract

Crème Pâtissière (see page 24)
or extra-thick custard flavoured
with chocolate, vanilla or crushed
hazelnuts, if liked, for filling

Put the butter, salt, sugar and 500ml/17fl oz/2 cups water in a large saucepan and bring to the boil. Remove from the heat, add the flour and mix to combine using a whisk. Return to a medium heat and stir gently with a wooden spoon until the mixture starts to dry and comes off the spoon easily and sweats slightly. Remove again from the heat and add the eggs one by one, whisking gently, until they are totally absorbed by the paste. You should have a lovely yellow, silky mixture. Stir in the vanilla extract and set the pastry aside to rest for 35–40 minutes.

Preheat the oven to 185°C/365°F/gas 4–5 and line a baking tray with baking parchment. Using a piping bag, pipe the pastry onto the baking tray to make 2.5cm/1in-thick balls. Bake for 20 minutes in the preheated oven, then turn the oven off and leave the profiteroles inside for another 10 minutes to dry them. They should be very light. Remove from the oven and transfer to a cooling rack to cool completely.

To fill the profiteroles, cut open from the bottom to the top, using a sharp knife, and pipe in the filling of your choice, such as crème pâtissière or extra-thick custard flavoured with chocolate, vanilla or crushed hazelnuts.

## *Crème anglaise*

# VANILLA CUSTARD

*Makes 1.4l/48fl oz/scant 6 cups*
*Preparation time 30 minutes*
*Cooking time 25 minutes*

1l/35fl oz/4 cups full fat milk

1 vanilla pod, halved lengthways

8 egg yolks

200g/7oz/heaped ¾ cup caster
  sugar

Put the milk in a medium saucepan over a low heat. Scrape the vanilla seeds into the milk, using a knife. Whisk, then throw in the vanilla pod as well. Simmer for at least 15 minutes to get the maximum flavour out of the seeds. Meanwhile, whisk the egg yolks and sugar together in a large bowl.

Add the egg-yolk mixture to the milk and cook over a medium heat for 5–8 minutes, stirring continuously (otherwise you will get scrambled eggs!) until it starts to thicken. You will be able to tell when it's ready if when you run 2 fingers down the back of the spoon the two lines don't immediately join. If the custard does start to scramble, don't panic – you can rescue it by pouring the mixture into a food processor, removing the vanilla pod, and blending it until it regains a smooth, thick texture. Strain immediately into a clean bowl and mix for a few minutes to cool the mixture down, then put it in the fridge to chill.

## *Crème pâtissière*

# CRÈME PÂTISSIÈRE

*Makes 750ml/26fl oz/3 cups*
*Preparation time 15 minutes*
*Cooking time 10–15 minutes*

500ml/17fl oz/2 cups full fat milk

1 vanilla pod, halved lengthways

5 egg yolks

100g/3½oz/scant ½ cup caster
  sugar

50g/1¾oz/heaped ¼ cup cornflour

small knob of butter

Put the milk in a medium saucepan over a low heat. Scrape the vanilla seeds into the milk, using a knife. Whisk, then throw in the vanilla pod as well. Heat the milk until it is almost simmering, remove from the heat and leave to infuse for about 20 minutes. Remove the vanilla pod from the milk and clean and dry in kitchen towel – you can use it again.

Meanwhile, whisk the egg yolks together with the sugar in a separate bowl until the mixture is light, thick and creamy and the sugar has dissolved. Gradually add the cornflour, a spoonful at a time, whisking well after each addition to avoid lumps.

Slowly pour half of the infused milk into the egg mixture, beating the mixture as you pour, then transfer the mixture back into the saucepan with the remaining milk. Place over a medium-low heat and stir continuously and quickly for about 10 minutes, or until the mixture begins to thicken. Remove from the heat and continue to stir until the mixture has cooled down and is lovely and smooth, thick and slightly trembling.

Pour into a container and rub a small knob of butter over – just enough to cover the top to avoid the surface drying out and forming a crust. Set aside until required. This is ideal for the Summer Fruit Tart on page 185.

## *Pâte à crêpes*
# BASIC CRÊPES

*Makes 12–15 crêpes*
*Preparation time 10 minutes*
*Cooking time 45 minutes*

125g/4½oz/1 cup plain flour

2 tbsp caster sugar

a few drops of vanilla extract

a pinch of salt

2 eggs

300ml/10½fl oz/scant 1¼ cups milk
(full fat or semi-skimmed)

30g/1oz butter, melted, plus extra
for frying, if needed

lemon juice and caster sugar, to
serve

Put the flour, sugar, vanilla extract, salt, eggs and 100ml/3½floz/scant ½ cup of the milk in a bowl. Add the butter and whisk until smooth. Alternatively, if it's easier for you, just pop everything into a blender. Blend for a few minutes, then slowly add the remaining milk and blend a little more. The important thing is to make sure that there are no lumps and the consistency is quite runny so that your crêpes will be thin and light. When you do it gradually like this, there is no need to rest the batter.

Heat a 15–18cm/6–7in non-stick pancake or frying pan over a medium-high heat. If you use a non-stick pan, you won't have to add butter to the pan as there is some already in the batter, though it can make the flipping easier if you do. If you're not using a non-stick pan, add a little butter to the pan first to keep the pancake from sticking.

Using a ladle, pour enough batter into the pan to cover the base thinly. Swirl the pan around to help spread the batter, if necessary, then cook for 1–1½ minutes. Now comes the fun part – try to flip it – or you can use a spatula. Cook for a further 1–2 minutes on the other side.

Remove the pancake from the pan and repeat with the remaining batter, adding more butter to the pan if necessary.

Sprinkle the pancakes with lemon juice and caster sugar, or any other topping you like such as jam, marmalade or ice cream. Enjoy!

Soupe de petits pois aux lardons

Caviar d'aubergine

Tapenade

Soupe à l'oignon gratinée au comté

Tomates séchées au four

Soupe de poisson avec mayonnaise au safran

Croque Monsieur au jambon et comté

## Les Entrées
# STARTERS

Starters are an important part of a meal in France, but they differ hugely from region to region. The recipes I've chosen here are specialities from all over the country. There is Duck Rillettes from the Dordogne, Fish Soup with Saffron Mayonnaise from the coastal regions or a selection of Tapenade and Aubergine Caviar from Provence, perhaps served with some cheese, charcuterie and crusty bread. With a glass of wine and good company, these entrées are a tantalizing treat to take you on to your dinner.

Soothing, velvety and rich, leek and potato soup is the ultimate comforting winter soup. If you want it to be very green, use small leeks and make sure you use the green part – lots of people throw this away thinking it is no good, but that is actually where the goodness and colour lie. To get rid of the grit and soil caught between layers, cut the leek into quarters lengthways from just above the root to the top – don't cut through the root. Fan out the layers and swirl them around in a bowl of water.

*Soupe de poireaux et pommes de terre aux champignons sauvages*

# LEEK & POTATO SOUP WITH WILD MUSHROOMS

*Preparation time 20 minutes, plus making the stock*
*Cooking time 30 minutes*

45g/1½oz butter

2 medium or 5 small leeks, diced and rinsed, keeping the white and green parts separate

2 large potatoes, peeled and diced

1 garlic clove, chopped

1 thyme sprig

1 shallot, peeled and chopped

500ml/17fl oz/2 cups Vegetable Stock (see page 19) or Chicken Stock (see page 18)

4 tbsp crème fraîche, plus extra to serve

85g/3oz wild or button mushrooms, sliced

1 tbsp chopped chives

sea salt and freshly ground black pepper

toasted baguette or farmhouse bread, to serve

Melt 30g/1oz of the butter gently in a large, heavy-based saucepan over a medium heat. Add the white part of the leeks and the potatoes, garlic, thyme and shallot and cook, partially covered, for 4–5 minutes. Stir occasionally, taking care not to let them colour. Add the stock and 250ml/9fl oz/1 cup water and season with salt. Bring to the boil, then reduce the heat to low and simmer for 15–20 minutes or until the potatoes are soft. Remove the thyme sprig.

Shortly before the potatoes have finished cooking, bring a medium saucepan of salted water to the boil. Add the green part of the leeks to the boiling water and blanch for 3–4 minutes, then drain, pour ice-cold water over them to seal in the colour and drain again. For maximum colour and a strong, earthy flavour, blanch the leeks just before blending with the potatoes. Transfer the blanched green leeks and the potato and leek mixture to a blender, season with salt and pepper and blend until very smooth, then add the crème fraîche. You may have to do this in batches, depending on the size of your blender. Pour the soup into a clean saucepan (straining it through a sieve if you want it really smooth) and keep warm over a low heat while you prepare the mushrooms.

Warm the remaining butter in a non-stick frying pan over a medium heat. When it is foaming, add the mushrooms, season with salt and pepper and cook, stirring occasionally, for 2 minutes or until golden brown. Remove from the heat and throw in the chives.

Put a spoonful of mushrooms in each bowl, pour the leek soup over them and top with a swirl of crème fraîche. Serve with bread. Creamy, simple and satisfying.

Wild garlic has a short season – about six weeks at the most – starting in early spring. You will find it in woodlands and alongside streams or canals, but if you can't go looking for it yourself, try your local farmers' markets. The smell is strong and distinctly garlicky, and the leaves look rather like spinach, only paler, and it is this combination that makes this a wonderfully tasty soup. The white flowers are also great in salads. When wild garlic is not in season, you can make this soup using spinach instead.

*Soupe d'ail sauvage*

# WILD GARLIC SOUP

*Preparation time 15 minutes, plus making the stock*
*Cooking time 25 minutes*

30g/1oz butter

1 small onion, chopped

1 large potato, peeled and chopped

875ml/30fl oz/3½ cups Vegetable Stock (see page 19) or Chicken Stock (see page 18)

600g/1lb 5oz wild garlic leaves

4 tbsp crème fraîche, or to taste, plus extra to serve

sea salt and freshly ground black pepper

Melt the butter in a medium saucepan over a low heat. Add the onion and cook for 4–5 minutes, stirring occasionally, until soft and pale without colour. Add the potato, season with salt and cook for 3–4 minutes, stirring so it does not stick to the bottom of the pan.

Add the stock, bring to the boil over a high heat, then reduce the heat to low and simmer for 10 minutes until the potato is soft. Add the wild garlic leaves and cook for another 5 minutes. You want to keep the colour, so don't overcook it.

Transfer the soup to a blender and blend until smooth. You may have to do this in batches, depending on the size of your blender. Add the crème fraîche, according to your taste, and season with salt and pepper. Serve warm, topped with an extra swirl of crème fraîche.

During the spring months, peas are one of my favourite vegetables. They seem underused in general, which is a pity because when cooked well they are so sweet and crunchy. Pea shoots add more depth of colour and flavour to this soup. They can be hard to find, although you can usually find them at farmers' markets or good supermarkets – it will definitely be worth your trouble. The freshness of peas combined with the rich saltiness of pancetta makes this a soup with style and substance.

*Soupe de petits pois aux lardons*

# PEA & PANCETTA SOUP

*Preparation time 20 minutes, plus making the stock*
*Cooking time 35 minutes*

30g/1oz butter

1 small leek, halved lengthways, rinsed and sliced

1 small potato, peeled and finely sliced

1–1.2l/35–40fl oz/4–5 cups Chicken Stock (see page 18) or Vegetable Stock (see page 19)

550g/1lb 4oz/3½ cups fresh or frozen peas

55g/2oz pea shoots (optional), plus extra to serve

4 tbsp double cream, plus extra to serve

85g/3oz pancetta, cut into strips

sea salt and freshly ground black pepper

farmhouse bread, to serve

Melt the butter in a medium saucepan over a low heat. Add the leek and potato and cook, stirring occasionally, for 5 minutes. Add the chicken stock and bring to the boil over a high heat, adjusting the amount of stock you add according to whether you like a thicker or thinner soup. Reduce the heat to low again and simmer for 10–12 minutes or until the potato is soft. Turn the heat down to its lowest setting and add the peas and pea shoots, if using. Simmer gently for 5 minutes, uncovered.

Transfer the mixture to a blender, season with salt and pepper and blend to the desired texture, adding the cream at the end. You may have to do this in batches depending on the size of your blender. Pour the soup into a clean saucepan (straining it through a sieve if you want it really smooth) and keep warm over a low heat while you prepare the pancetta.

Bring a small saucepan of water to the boil. Add the pancetta, return to the boil and then remove from the heat. This will remove excess fat and salt. Drain and pat dry on kitchen towel. Heat a non-stick frying pan over a medium heat, add the pancetta and fry for 4–5 minutes, tossing until crispy.

Put a spoonful of pancetta in each bowl and pour the soup over it. Add a swirl of cream and a sprig of pea shoots, if using, and serve with bread – a lovely spring soup.

During spring and summer, wild watercress can be found in abundance alongside streams and rivers. Young watercress leaves are softer and less bitter, so try to get these if you can. This soup has a deep, herb-green colour and a delicate, grassy flavour, and it is full of goodness. The key to keeping the colour is to cook it very gently and for a short time. The finished result should be smooth in texture, rich in colour and peppery in taste. For an extra special touch, serve with a poached quail egg on a slice of toasted baguette.

*Soupe de cresson de fontaine et pommes de terre, oeuf de caille sur croûtons*

# WATERCRESS & POTATO SOUP WITH QUAIL EGG CROÛTONS

*Preparation time 25 minutes*
*Cooking time 30 minutes*

30g/1oz butter

2 shallots, chopped

1 large leek, sliced and rinsed

350g/12oz potatoes, peeled and diced

300g/10½oz watercress, stalks removed

4 tbsp double cream, plus extra to serve

1 baguette

1 tsp vinegar

4 quail eggs

sea salt and ground white pepper

Melt the butter in a medium saucepan over a low heat. Add the shallots and leek and cook, stirring occasionally, for 3–4 minutes, then add the potatoes and enough boiling water to cover generously, about 750ml/26fl oz/3 cups. Simmer for 10–12 minutes or until the potatoes are soft. Remove from the heat, add the watercress, cover and set aside for 4–5 minutes.

Transfer the mixture to a blender, season with salt and pepper and blend until smooth, adding the cream at the end. Don't be shy with the seasoning, as watercress can take quite a lot. If you like your soup with a finer texture, strain it through a sieve into a clean saucepan and warm through – very gently or the chlorophyll will break down and the soup will lose its fabulous, vibrant colour.

Toast 4 slices of baguette. Bring a small saucepan of water to a gentle simmer, then add the vinegar. Carefully break the quail eggs, one at a time, into the water and poach for 1–2 minutes – the egg yolks should remain soft. Remove the eggs using a slotted spoon and rest the spoon on kitchen paper. Carefully pat dry the eggs. Put a warm, toasted bread slice in each bowl, top each with a poached egg and pierce the eggs so the yolk runs down into the soup bowl. Pour the soup into the bowl around the baguette slice, add a swirl of cream and serve with the remaining baguette.

Like the sea itself, this soup is powerful and aromatic. When I eat it, it makes me think of standing on a high rock, breathing in the salty sea air. Rockfish are found in brasseries in coastal villages and cities from Marseille to Bordeaux to Brest. Fish soups differ according not only to the variety of fish used but also where they are caught – fish from warm water will have a different flavour from fish from cold water, for example. In France, the type of fish used will be typical to the area and most likely true to a recipe that has been passed down from generation to generation or from chef to chef. Either way, everyone will claim that theirs is best!

*Soupe de poisson avec mayonnaise au safran*

# FISH SOUP WITH SAFFRON MAYONNAISE

*Preparation time 20 minutes, plus making the mayonnaise*
*Cooking time 1 hour 10 minutes*

4 tbsp olive oil

4 garlic cloves, crushed

1 fennel bulb, chopped

2 onions, sliced

4 small soft shell crabs (optional)

800g/1lb 12oz small rockfish, such as monkfish and red or grey mullet, scaled, gutted and gills removed (you can ask your fishmonger to do this)

4 tbsp aniseed liqueur, such as Pastis or Pernod

200g/7oz tomatoes, chopped

55g/2oz/scant ¼ cup tomato purée

1 bay leaf

a pinch of saffron powder

a pinch of cayenne pepper

sea salt and freshly ground black pepper

croûtons, to serve

½ recipe quantity Saffron Mayonnaise (see page 21), to serve

Warm the oil in a large, deep frying pan or cast iron pan over a medium heat. Add the garlic, fennel and onions and cook, stirring often to avoid discolouring, for 3–5 minutes until soft.

Add the crabs, if using, and cook for 4–5 minutes until the shells become red. Add the rockfish and cook over a medium-high heat for a further 5 minutes, stirring to make sure it doesn't stick to the bottom. Add the Pastis, tomatoes, tomato purée, bay leaf, saffron, cayenne pepper and 2l/70fl oz/8 cups water. Bring to the boil, then reduce the heat to medium and cook for 50 minutes. After that time, the flesh should have come away from the fish bones. Remove and discard the bones.

Transfer the soup to a blender and blend until smooth. It will be a little thick, but that is exactly how you want it. Strain it through a sieve, if desired, into a clean saucepan, reheat and season with salt and pepper.

Serve with croûtons and saffron mayonnaise.

This soup is at the heart of French cooking. It is made in homes and brasseries right across France and loved by all. You will need some really good onions, like the white ones from Provence or your local farmer's supply. Being from Franche-Comté, I think this dish tastes best when the croûtons are made with the famous Comté cheese. The combination of rich, golden cheese melting into the tangy, glistening onions makes it second to none. A great one to keep on the stove to share with a friend after a night out.

*Soupe à l'oignon gratinée au comté*

# ONION SOUP WITH COMTÉ CHEESE

*Preparation time 30 minutes*
*Cooking time 45 minutes*

85g/3oz butter

6 onions, sliced

2 tbsp plain flour

4 tbsp red wine

100ml/3½fl oz/scant ½ cup white wine

1 tsp sugar (optional)

4 thick slices baguette

2 tbsp olive oil

150g/5½oz Comté cheese, grated

sea salt and freshly ground black pepper

Melt the butter in a large saucepan over a low heat. Add the onions, season with salt and pepper and cook, partially covered, for 10 minutes or until they are a golden colour. Stir often so they don't burn. Sprinkle with the flour and cook for a further 10 minutes until the onions start to brown.

In a heatproof jug, mix together the wines and 1.75l/60fl oz/7 cups boiling water, then slowly pour the mixture over the onions, stirring continuously to prevent lumps. Bring to the boil over a high heat, skimming away any impurities from the surface, then reduce the heat to low and simmer for 15–20 minutes. Taste the soup and adjust the salt and pepper. If it seems too sour, add a little sugar to taste.

Meanwhile, to make the cheesy croûtons, preheat the grill to high. Put the baguette slices on a baking tray, drizzle with the olive oil and sprinkle with the grated cheese. Grill for 4–5 minutes or until the cheese is melted and golden brown, being careful not to burn the edges of the baguette.

Divide the soup into bowls, pop the croûtons on top and enjoy. If it is less than heavenly, I want to know why!

CHEF'S TIP: *The traditional way to make this soup is with water, as I've done here, however, if you want a richer soup you can replace the water with either vegetable or chicken stock. You could also serve it with garlic croûtons, if liked. Instead of melting cheese on the baguette, drizzle the slices with olive oil, lightly toast them under the grill and then rub with garlic cloves that you've cut in half to release maximum flavour.*

# *Les Pains*
# **Breads**

For me, bread has always been significant not only because I love it but also because it goes so well with so many other foods, such as cheese, pâté, charcuterie, hot and cold meats and much more.

Bread is close to a religion in France. All over the country bakeries (*boulangeries*) take turns so that there is always one open every day of the week. On Saturdays and Sundays they are open all day. The best-known French bread of all, the classic baguette (meaning 'stick' in French) is the only bread to be sold at a fixed price across France because the government considers it essential to life! New batches appear on shelves all day long because it should always be eaten fresh, and can go chewy very quickly. You often see people riding bikes or on trains with a baguette under their arm.

The breaking of bread is a great gesture that has no equal around the table, one that creates a sense of sharing and friendship, whether it's a simple baguette or *boule* (round-shaped, generally white bread, available in different sizes and types of flours), a *pain de campagne* (a rustic loaf with a thick crust and one of the most popular farmhouse breads) or more exotic types such as *pain aux noix* (bread made with nuts), *pain aux raisins* (bread made with raisins) or *fougasse* (a *focaccia*-type bread, very popular in the South of France.)

Most traditional versions of *pain de campagne* are made with a mixture of white, wholemeal and/or rye flour, water, leavening and salt. Cut in diagonals and served with charcuterie and gherkins, there's nothing better. Pain aux noix is delicious with foie gras and both *pain aux noix* and *pain aux raisins* go extremely well with cheese. *Fougasse* is often made with bacon (*aux lardons*), onions (*aux oignons*), herbs (*aux herbes*), olives (*aux olives*) or anchovies (*aux anchois*). You probably wouldn't set out to buy these breads, but when you see them on display, you can't resist them! Before you know it you have bought the cheese to go with them, and maybe some wine too, and you have a perfect impromptu meal!

In France, it seems that everyone has their own favourite baker. In small villages and in towns like mine the *boulangerie* is always a rendez-vous for locals where they can chat about anything and everything and usually, by the time they've finished, they realize they've finished the baguette too, so they have to go back to buy another one!

As a child, I often used to do the shopping. When I was very young and not that tall, I could not reach the counter in some shops, so I would just hand over the note Maman had written for me and be given whatever food we were having that day for lunch or dinner. My last shop was always the baker, where I'd pick up one or two baguettes and one 'long bread' (a longer version of the baguette).

Another popular baguette variation is the *ficelle* (French for 'string' because it is thin), which is generally used for quick snacks. As children we used to love to put a bar of dark chocolate in our *ficelle* for our *quatre heures* – our after-school snack. We also enjoyed *pain de mie*, a soft semi-sweet loaf with a thin crust, mainly used for sandwiches; *pain au lait*, a sweet roll that is very moist and easy to eat because it has no crust, and *pain de seigle*, made from two-thirds rye flour, one-third wheat flour – a tasty alternative to baguette, and great with cheese or charcuterie.

On the way home from shopping trips, I'd start eating one of the baguettes, sometimes devouring more than half. It was still warm and tasted so good that I simply could not resist it. The smell used to tempt me so much, just as it did when I entered the bakery right after bread had been baked, or *croissants* and *pains au chocolat* had just come out of the oven. It is those moments I cannot forget and which I love to experience again when I go back home. It's wonderful to hold the bread to your ear and slowly crush it so that it crackles at the same time that it releases its warm, just-baked aroma! How could I ever *not* eat bread?

But real bread is in danger. Mass-produced bread is in demand. Quickly made with fast-growing crops, such bread is often too heavy, very poor in natural nutrients and filled with yeast substitutes. Simple, good, healthy bread, made naturally, is what we should be eating. Long live the traditional bakers, masters of their trade, passionate about their art, working all night to ensure that their faithful clients remain the same and spread the word.

I have always considered the art of baking, along with the other culinary arts, to be a very noble profession, where you create wonderful food with your own hands. In this book, you will find recipes where bread is central and other ingredients complement it, not the other way around. There are the delicious Croque Monsieur and Croque Madame, made from day-old bread, toasted farmhouse bread with *rillettes* or croûtons in onion soup, and many more. Always buy good bread to serve with your meals and don't compromise on ingredients. Find a good baker and freeze the loaves so you can always enjoy tasty bread. Or, if you make your own, use a reputable flour, organic if possible (or, even better, stone-ground), and buy it high-quality, not bleached. Then, using good yeast, you will get a great result that is much healthier for your family.

## A BRIEF HISTORY OF BREAD

Humans have been making bread for at least 8,000 years, but it wasn't always good to eat. Early, unleavened versions were cooked on a slate stone, which made the bread so tough that you could lose your teeth eating it! A 4,000-year-old sample on display at London's British Museum is proof of how far the craft of bread-baking has come.

Legend has it that we owe our modern-day bread to a young Egyptian who once forgot to cook his dough. After a while, it began to ferment and the yeast cultures that are naturally found in flour became active. When he eventually did cook it, the dough rose, becoming the first leavened bread. Today, artisan bakers in France often produce their own yeast for leavened bread by preparing a 'growth culture', which they constantly refresh, so it provides leavening for years. It gives the bread a special flavour and texture. This *pain au levain* (traditionally leavened bread) is generally bought as a massive *boule* (ball), cut into long slices and served with butter.

The Egyptians were expert wheat growers, and sold their excess crop to the Greeks, who went on to develop the bread-making technique further. The Romans then learned from them. They created a school for bakers, and by the year 100BC there were said to be 258 bakeries in Rome. It is believed that the Emperor Cassius brought the first bread to Britain. Rotary millstones and watermills were built soon afterwards to enable locals to produce their own flour and bread. But when the Romans left Britain, so did the baking knowledge ... until the Normans arrived and revived the yeasted loaf.

Now, as you can see, we have been making bread in Britain for a long time and it hasn't always been cheap or, I should say, good value. In the 19th century, the tax on imported wheat was so high that a single loaf cost a person's entire wages and the people revolted. The tax was abolished in 1846.

The 20th century saw the start of the mass production of bread. More bread was made faster, but unfortunately the process compromised both its quality and nutritional content. The domestic bread-making machine arrived at the end of the century, making it easier for home cooks to bake their own bread – and with very good results, too. Once upon a time, the wealthier you were, the whiter your bread. Today, the emphasis is on wholemeal grains, and the browner breads are the healthier choice.

LEFT PAGE CLOCKWISE FROM TOP LEFT:
pain de campagne rond, pain de campagne long, baguette paysanne, pain paysan, fougasse, fougasse aux céréales, pain de Meule

RIGHT PAGE CLOCKWISE FROM LEFT:
baguette artisanale, ficelle, ficelle aux céréales, pain artisanal, pain de campagne aux noix, pain de mie

The word tapenade comes from the Provençal word 'tapeno', meaning capers, which are the traditional base for this tantalizing combination. You can make it in many different ways according to your taste, and some recipes from Provence use a larger proportion of capers to olives, but the one I like is made with black olives (from the South of France, if possible) and watercress leaves. It is a beautiful deep purple colour and full of flavour and complexity. It tastes great with crudités, on toasted bread with fresh tomatoes, or even served alongside roast lamb or chicken.

*Tapenade*

# TAPENADE

*Preparation time 10 minutes*

175g/6oz/1½ cups small pitted black olives

1 tinned anchovy fillet (optional)

125ml/4fl oz/½ cup olive oil

1 garlic clove

1 handful of watercress leaves, stalks discarded

1 tbsp capers, rinsed

Put all the ingredients in a food processor and process for 3–4 minutes until the mixture forms a paste of the desired consistency.

Transfer to a small jar (the one the olives came in would be ideal), cover with a lid and keep in the fridge. The tapenade will keep for up to 2 weeks and will be better than anything you could buy in the shops!

**VARIATION:** GREEN OLIVE TAPENADE
If you want to try a variation, replace the black olives with green ones and replace the watercress with 1 handful of basil leaves.

*Anchoïade*

# ANCHOÏADE

*Preparation time 15 minutes*

200g/7oz salted anchovy fillets

2 garlic cloves

1 tsp white wine vinegar

150ml/5fl oz/scant ⅔ cup olive oil

freshly ground black pepper

Rinse the anchovy fillets well under cold running water, then pat dry using a clean tea towel.

Put the anchovy fillets, garlic and vinegar in a mortar or small food processor and season with pepper. Work everything together with the pestle or by processing until the mixture forms a paste. Slowly add the oil while continuing to mix. You should end up with a smooth, silky texture.

Transfer the anchoïade to a small jar, cover with a lid and keep in the fridge. It will keep for up to 2 weeks.

*Tomates séchées au four*

# OVEN-DRIED TOMATOES

*Preparation time 10 minutes*
*Cooking time 3 hours*

90ml/3fl oz/⅓ cup olive oil, plus
    extra as needed

6 garlic cloves, unpeeled and
    crushed with the flat edge of
    a knife or your hand

500g/1lb 2oz cherry tomatoes

2 tsp icing sugar

a few thyme or rosemary sprigs

sea salt and freshly ground black
    pepper

Preheat the oven to 110°C/225°F/gas ½. Put the oil and garlic in a small baking dish and leave to infuse in the oven for 30 minutes, then remove the garlic. This will give you a lovely scented oil in which to roast your tomatoes. (Don't waste the garlic: once you've got the tomatoes in the oven toast some crusty bread, drizzle it with olive oil and eat it with the garlic – which you can push out from its skin – it's incredible!)

Cut the tomatoes in half, across the middle rather than from top to bottom (they somehow look more appealing cut this way). Squeeze gently to remove some of the seeds and juice so they will dry more easily, then put them skin-side down in the baking dish. Put the icing sugar in a fine sieve and sprinkle it over the tomatoes, then season with salt and pepper. Toss the thyme sprigs over them and leave in the oven to dry for 2½ hours. Serve warm or leave to cool and then remove the thyme sprigs, put the tomatoes in a jar and cover them with extra olive oil. They will keep in the fridge for 2–3 weeks.

*Caviar d'aubergine*

# AUBERGINE CAVIAR

*Preparation time 15 minutes*
*Cooking time 1 hour*

3 aubergines, halved lengthways

90ml/3fl oz/⅓ cup olive oil, plus
    extra as needed

6 garlic cloves, unpeeled and
    crushed with the flat edge of
    a knife or your hand

6 thyme or rosemary sprigs

sea salt and freshly ground black
    pepper

Preheat the oven to 180°C/350°F/gas 4. Using a sharp knife, score the flesh of the aubergines, making a crisscross pattern. Put them on a baking tray, flesh-side up, drizzle with the oil and season with salt and pepper. Put 1 garlic clove and 1 thyme sprig on each aubergine half, cover with foil and bake for 1 hour or until the aubergines are very soft and the flesh is easy to scoop out.

Remove from the oven and discard the thyme. Peel the garlic cloves and put them on a chopping board. Scoop the flesh from the aubergines onto the chopping board and discard the skins. Chop finely, mixing in the garlic, then season with salt and pepper and add a drop of oil, if liked.

Transfer the caviar to a jar, cover the surface with extra oil and cover with a lid. It will keep for up to 1 week in the fridge.

You find yourself in Paris for a weekend, the sun is shining and you manage to get a seat on a terrace outside a brasserie on one of the wide boulevards. You are thinking you would like to watch the world go by for an hour or two and soak up the atmosphere. Maybe you'll have a snack … but what? No trip to Paris would be complete without a Croque Monsieur. This is a twist on the traditional, call it Croque Monsieur Galmiche if you will. It is the way we used to do it at home – our Sunday night treat.

*Croque Monsieur au jambon et comté*

# CROQUE MONSIEUR WITH HAM & COMTÉ CHEESE

*Preparation time 15 minutes, plus making the salad and vinaigrette*
*Cooking time 5 minutes*

4 large eggs

400ml/14fl oz/scant 1⅔ cups full-fat milk

1 long *pain paysan* (or a farmhouse loaf bread), cut diagonally into 8 thick slices

150g/5½oz butter

8 slices of ham

100g/3½oz aged Comté cheese or other mature hard cheese, grated

sea salt and freshly ground black pepper

lamb's lettuce salad tossed with French Vinaigrette (see page 20), to serve

Put the eggs and milk in a bowl, season with salt and pepper and whisk well, then transfer to a shallow dish. Soak each slice of bread in the egg mixture, turning three or four times so that it really takes in the liquid.

Melt half the butter in a large frying pan over a medium heat. When foaming, add the bread and cook for 2 minutes until golden brown and a little crispy, then turn the bread over and add the rest of the butter. Cook on the other side for 2 minutes. If you are using a small frying pan, cook in batches using a quarter of the butter for each batch.

Put 1 slice of ham and some of the grated cheese on each slice of bread, and when the cheese starts to melt add another slice of bread on top of the cheese and flick the croque monsieur over once more and cook for up to 1 minute until heated through. Serve hot with lamb's lettuce salad. Perfect!

A creamier, richer alternative for Madame, with the simple addition of a fried egg and a couple of spoonfuls of Béchamel sauce. Béchamel sauce owes its name to the Marquis of Béchamel, who felt it was an improvement on velouté (which is made in a similar way but with white stock rather than milk), although it was originally made by simply adding large quantities of cream.

## *Croque Madame*
# CROQUE MADAME

*Preparation time 5 minutes, plus making the Croque Monsieur and 20 minutes chilling*
*Cooking time 15 minutes*

40g/1½oz butter, softened

40g/1½oz/⅓ cup plain flour

400ml/14fl oz/scant 1⅔ cups milk

a pinch of freshly grated nutmeg

1 tbsp sunflower oil

4 eggs

1 recipe quantity Croque Monsieur with Ham & Comté Cheese (see page 42)

sea salt and freshly ground black pepper

In a small bowl, mix the butter and flour together until the mixture forms a smooth paste, cover with cling film and chill for 20 minutes.

Put the milk and nutmeg in a saucepan and season with salt and pepper. Bring to the boil, then remove from the heat and set aside to infuse and cool for about 15 minutes.

Gently reheat the milk over a medium-low heat and add the butter and flour paste, little by little, until the milk thickens to a sauce. Stir continuously to make sure you get a lovely smooth texture without any lumps. This is known as a béchamel sauce.

Preheat the grill to medium-high. Meanwhile, make your Croque Monsieur according to the recipe instructions.

To fry the eggs, heat a large frying pan over a medium heat, then add the sunflower oil. When it starts to smoke, break the eggs into the pan, without bursting the yolks, and fry until the whites are cooked and the edges crispy and golden.

Put 1 egg on top of each Croque Monsieur and pour a few spoonfuls of the béchamel sauce over each one. Grill for 3–4 minutes or until light golden.

Leeks make a great alternative to asparagus when it is out of season. These tasty vegetables belong to the same family as onions and garlic but have a milder flavour, which works really well in this dish with vinaigrette. If you're using bigger, older leeks, cut the coarse, green part away and use only the white part. But if you've opted for younger, baby leeks, you can use the whole vegetable.

*Poireaux à la vinaigrette*

# LEEKS WITH VINAIGRETTE

*Preparation time 10 minutes, plus making the vinaigrette*
*Cooking time 20 minutes*

1 tsp vinegar

2 eggs, at room temperature

4 leeks or 12 baby leeks

1 small handful of flat-leaf parsley, chopped

1 recipe quantity French Vinaigrette (see page 20)

sea salt

Fill a small saucepan with water and bring to the boil. Add the vinegar to the water, as this will make the eggs easier to shell after cooking. Place the eggs in a ladle, then slowly and carefully slide the eggs into the water so that you don't break the shells. Cook for 8–9 minutes, drain and place the eggs under running cold water. When cool enough to handle, shell the eggs, roughly chop and set aside.

Bring a medium saucepan of salted water to the boil. Add the leeks and cook over a medium heat for 15 minutes. Drain and immediately plunge the leeks directly into cold water for a few seconds to stop the cooking process and keep the bright colour. Don't leave them in the water for too long, because you want them still to be warm. Pat the leeks dry on a clean tea towel, then arrange on a flat serving dish.

Mix the chopped eggs and parsley into the vinaigrette, pour the mixture over the leeks and serve. Colourful, simple and delicious.

CHEF'S TIP: *When hard- or soft-boiling eggs, it is best to use the eggs at room temperature and not directly from the fridge, when the shells are more likely to crack as you add them to the boiling water.*

Late spring is the season of asparagus, both green and white; the best is whatever you can buy locally. Asparagus has quite a short season of seven or eight weeks, so make the most of this luxurious vegetable when it's available. I like to keep the flavours simple, such as in this dish, so you can really appreciate its freshness! The question with asparagus is always where to cut it; the way you can tell is by holding it from both ends and bending it – the spear will naturally snap between your fingers at just the right place.

*Asperges à la vinaigrette au persil*

# ASPARAGUS WITH PARSLEY VINAIGRETTE

*Preparation time 15 minutes*
*Cooking time 20 minutes*

500g/1lb 2oz asparagus, woody ends discarded, peeled if tough

1 tbsp sea salt

**PARSLEY VINAIGRETTE**

2 tbsp white wine vinegar, plus extra to hard-boil the egg

1 egg, at room temperature

2 tsp Dijon mustard

100ml/3½fl oz/scant ½ cup sunflower or olive oil

1 small handful of parsley, chopped

sea salt and freshly ground black pepper

Fill a small saucepan with water and bring to the boil. Add a teaspoon of vinegar to the water, as this will make the egg easier to shell after cooking. Place the egg in a ladle, then slowly and carefully slide the egg into the water so that you don't break the shell. Cook for 8–9 minutes, drain and place the egg under running cold water. When cool enough to handle, shell the egg, chop roughly and set aside.

Bring a medium saucepan of water to the boil and add the salt. Tie up the asparagus loosely with string, tips all facing the same way, and put the bundle in the pan. Reduce the heat to low and cook for 6–10 minutes, depending on the size of the asparagus. The spears should be cooked through but still retain some bite.

Meanwhile, prepare a bowl of ice-cold water and set aside and make the parsley vinaigrette. Put the mustard and vinegar in a bowl, season with salt and pepper and mix well. Slowly whisk or beat in the oil, then stir in the chopped egg and parsley.

When the asparagus is cooked, remove the bundle from the pan and plunge it into the ice-cold water. This helps to keep the chlorophyll (and therefore the goodness and colour) locked in.

Drain the asparagus, untie and arrange it on a flat dish. Pour the vinaigrette over and serve. This is a great dish to share with a friend, using nothing but your fingers – at least that is how we do it in France!

Asparagus, poached egg and hollandaise sauce – the perfect *ménage à trois*! Of course, you can often get hold of asparagus throughout the year, but it is always better when in season. Green works better than white for this dish, and rich, glossy, home-made hollandaise makes more difference than I can say.

*Oeuf poché aux asperges et sauce hollandaise*

# POACHED EGG WITH ASPARAGUS & HOLLANDAISE SAUCE

*Preparation time 10 minutes, plus making the sauce*
*Cooking time 15 minutes*

1kg/2lb 4oz small to medium green asparagus spears, woody ends discarded, peeled if tough

4 tbsp white wine vinegar

4 large eggs

sea salt and freshly ground black pepper

1 recipe quantity Hollandaise Sauce (see page 20)

Bring a saucepan of salted water to the boil. Tie up the asparagus loosely with string, tips all facing the same way, and put the bundle in the pan. Reduce the heat to low and cook for 6–10 minutes, depending on the size of your asparagus. The spears should be cooked through but still retain some bite.

Meanwhile, prepare a bowl of ice-cold water and set aside. Bring another small saucepan of water to the boil, add the vinegar and bring it down to a simmer. Break 2 of the eggs into the pan (or just do one at a time if you still don't feel confident about poaching eggs). Swirl the water a little and keep simmering for 4 minutes or until the white surrounds the yolk in a nice oval shape (you can manipulate it, using a spoon). Alternatively, if you have an egg poacher, you can just use that.

When the asparagus is cooked, remove the bundle from the pan and plunge it into the ice-cold water. This helps to keep the chlorophyll (and therefore the goodness and colour) locked in.

Untie the asparagus and divide it onto four plates. Top each portion with a poached egg, then with a dollop of the hollandaise sauce, so it just runs down the side of the egg on to the asparagus. Season with salt and pepper and serve immediately. I promise you, it's wonderful!

## *Crabe tiède avec mayonnaise à l'estragon*

# WARM CRAB WITH TARRAGON MAYONNAISE

*Preparation time 10 minutes, plus
making the vinaigrette
Cooking time 3 minutes*

100g/3½oz cooked crab meat

4 tbsp mayonnaise

1 small handful of tarragon,
chopped

3–4 drops of chilli sauce

sea salt and freshly ground black
pepper

seasonal mixed leaves, to serve

1 avocado, peeled, pitted and sliced,
to serve

1 recipe quantity French Vinaigrette
(see page 20) made with coarse
mustard instead of Dijon mustard.

Put the crab meat in a heatproof bowl and rest it over a saucepan of gently simmering water, making sure the bottom of the bowl does not touch the water. Heat over a low heat for 2–3 minutes, to warm the crab meat through, then remove from the heat and mix in the mayonnaise, tarragon and chilli sauce and season with salt and pepper.

Serve warm with mixed leaves and sliced avocado, drizzled with the vinaigrette.

## *Filet de maquereau au citron vert*

# MACKEREL WITH LIME (PICTURED)

*Preparation time 30 minutes, plus
1 hour marinating
Cooking time 7 minutes*

2 whole mackerel, about 400g/14oz
each, filleted

4 tbsp olive oil

1 kaffir lime leaf, cut into fine strips

a pinch of sea salt

a pinch of freshly ground black
pepper

1 lime, halved

Score the filleted mackerel slightly so that the marinade can really penetrate the flesh and put them in a small dish. Add all the remaining ingredients except for the lime, cover with cling film and leave to marinate for 1 hour in the fridge.

Preheat the oven to 180°C/350°F/gas 4. Heat a small frying pan over a medium-high heat. Put the fish, skin-side down, on the pan and fry for 2 minutes to give it a nice colour, then transfer it to a baking tray and bake for 5 minutes.

Squeeze the lime over the mackerel and serve.

You can find this popular traditional dish on tables in almost every region of France, and in quite a few supermarkets, too – but it is never quite the same as home-made. There are so many recipes for what is known simply as 'pâté' – but you need the right balance of liver and fat to make it both smooth and tasty, and some recipes have a very high percentage of fat, which isn't necessary or good for you. Pâté is complemented simply and beautifully by gherkins, pickled vegetables and farmhouse bread, making it a great dish for outdoor family gatherings.

*Terrine de foie de volaille*

# CHICKEN LIVER TERRINE

*Preparation time 30 minutes, plus overnight soaking, 3 hours cooling and 2 days resting*
*Cooking time 1 hour 5 minutes*

500g/1lb 2oz chicken livers, trimmed by your butcher, all green parts removed

1l/35fl oz/4 cups milk

1 tbsp sea salt

4 tbsp crème fraîche

1 garlic clove, crushed

a pinch of freshly grated nutmeg

2 tbsp Cognac

4 eggs

4 egg yolks

75g/2½oz/scant ⅔ cup cornflour

150g/5½oz butter

sea salt and ground white pepper

gherkins, to serve

pickled vegetables, to serve

warm toasted bread or farmhouse bread, to serve

Put the livers in a large bowl and cover with 250ml/9fl oz/1 cup of the milk and 250ml/9fl oz/1 cup water. Sprinkle with the salt and leave to marinate in the fridge overnight, or for at least 2 hours. Drain the livers, rinse under running water and put them on a clean tea towel to remove any excess liquid. Put the crème fraîche, garlic, nutmeg and remaining milk in a medium saucepan. Season with salt and white pepper and warm over a low heat for 5 minutes.

Preheat the oven to 130°C/250°F/gas 1. Put the livers and Cognac in a blender and blend for 20–30 seconds. Add the eggs, egg yolks and cornflour and blend for a further 5 minutes until smooth and silky. While the blender is running, gradually add the milk mixture, a little at a time, covering the blender with the lid between additions and continuing to blend until all the liquid is incorporated.

Strain the mixture through a sieve into a 24 x 10 x 8cm/9½ x 4 x 3¼in terrine mould (preferably cast iron) and cover with a piece of greaseproof paper the size of the terrine. Put the terrine in a deep baking dish and fill the dish with enough hot water to come two-thirds of the way up the sides of the mould. Bake for 1 hour. The terrine is done when a knife inserted into it comes out dry and hot if tested on sensitive skin such as the inside of your wrist. Alternatively, a thermometer inserted into the centre reads around 68°C/154°F. Leave the terrine to cool for at least 2–3 hours.

Melt the butter and pour it over the top to prevent oxidation. Cover with cling film and leave for 2 days in the fridge to allow the terrine to set and the flavours to concentrate. To serve, dip a knife in hot water and run it along the sides of the terrine mould, then put the mould in water for 1 minute to help loosen it further before unmoulding it onto a plate. Slice and serve with gherkins, pickled vegetables and warm, toasted bread.

Contrary to what people think, making a terrine isn't difficult, but it does take time – you usually need to make it at least two days in advance to ensure that the flavours really develop and it sets properly. This recipe can be easily adapted to use game during the hunting season, if you like. It is also delicious made with young wild boar, pheasant, partridge, wild duck or deer.

*Terrine de porc*

# PORK TERRINE

*Preparation time 35 minutes, plus overnight marinating and 2 days resting*
*Cooking time 1 hour 30 minutes*

300g/10½oz pork shoulder, cut into 2.5/1in cubes

300g/10½oz pork liver, minced

300g/10½oz pork neck, half cut into 2.5cm/1in cubes and half minced

300g/10½oz pork fat from belly, minced

3 tbsp Armagnac

½ teaspoon freshly grated nutmeg

100ml/3½fl oz/scant ½ cup dry white wine

¾ teaspoon salt

½ teaspoon ground white pepper

12 slices of smoked streaky bacon

2 eggs

100ml/3½fl oz/scant ½ cup double cream

35g/1¼oz/¼ cup shelled unsalted pistachio nuts

2 thyme sprigs

pickled vegetables, to serve

warm toasted bread, to serve

Twenty-four hours before cooking, chop the pork shoulder, pork liver, pork neck and pork fat until you have a coarse mince texture, or pulse in a food processor. If using a food processor, process one ingredient at a time before transferring it to a large mixing bowl. Mix in the Armagnac, nutmeg, wine, salt and white pepper, then cover with cling film and marinate in the fridge overnight. If time doesn't allow, chill for at least 3 hours.

Preheat the oven to 130°C/250°F/gas 1 and remove the bowl from the fridge. Cover the base and sides of a 24 x 10 x 8cm/9½ x 4 x 3¼in terrine mould with the bacon, allowing it to hang over the sides, and set aside.

Now it is time to finish the terrine mix. Whisk the eggs and cream together and gradually mix them into the meat, using a spatula. Once thoroughly mixed, add the pistachios. Transfer to the terrine mould (preferably cast iron) and pack the mixture down by pressing with the spatula or the back of a spoon. Put the thyme sprigs on top and cover with the overlapping bacon. Put the terrine in a deep baking dish and fill the dish with enough hot water to come two-thirds of the way up the sides of the terrine mould. Bake for 1½ hours.

The terrine is done when a thermometer inserted into the centre reads around 68°C/154°F. Alternatively, insert a knife into the terrine. It should come out dry and hot if tested on sensitive skin such as the inside of your wrist or your lip.

Leave the terrine to cool completely at room temperature with a 1–2kg/2lb 4oz–4lb 8oz weight, such as a bag of sugar, on top. Place a piece of greaseproof paper between the terrine and the weight. Once cold, cover and leave in the fridge for 2 days before serving to allow the flavours to develop. This resting time will really enhance the flavour. Serve with pickled vegetables and bread.

Rillettes are prepared from cooked, shredded meat and are served in ways similar to pâté. Ready-made rillettes are widely available from delicatessens, but they are also easy to make yourself – with the bonus that you also get to use the meat or poultry of your choice. As well as the traditional pork belly, you can make rillettes from duck, goose, rabbit or even wild boar. Served with toasted baguette and other charcuterie, they make an ideal starter.

*Rillettes de canard*

# DUCK RILLETTES

*Preparation time 30 minutes, plus overnight marinating and 1 day resting*
*Cooking time 6 hours*

8 large duck legs, 150g/5½oz each

60g/2¼oz/¼ cup sea salt

3 bay leaves

5 thyme sprigs, lightly crushed

1.5kg/3lb 5oz goose fat

a few whole black peppercorns (optional)

freshly ground black pepper

crusty bread, to serve

Put the duck legs in a bowl, skin-side down. Add the salt, 2 of the bay leaves and 4 of the thyme sprigs and season with pepper. Toss well, then cover with cling film and marinate in the fridge overnight or for at least 2 hours. The longer you leave the duck to marinate the more flavour your dish will have.

Preheat the oven to 130°C/250°F/gas 1. Briefly rinse the duck legs under cold running water to remove the excess salt, then drain on kitchen towel.

Melt the goose fat in a large cast iron casserole dish over a low heat. Add the duck and toss until well coated, then transfer to the preheated oven, uncovered, and cook without stirring for 6 hours until the meat is falling easily from the bone. Remove the duck legs from the pan, discard the skin and bones and shred the meat into a mixing bowl, using a fork. Mix in a little of the warm goose fat to moisten.

Transfer the mixture to a sealable jar, or to a small earthenware dish, and press it down. Pour a film of goose fat over the top to seal it, then top with the remaining thyme sprig and bay leaf and a few whole peppercorns, if liked. Cover with greaseproof paper and refrigerate for at least 24 hours before using to enhance the flavour. The remaining goose fat can be put in a jar and kept for other uses.

Serve with crusty bread.

As an alternative to my classic Goat's Cheese Salad below, you could also try this even simpler version – it's full of wonderful flavours! Simply stop at the supermarket and pick up a selection of green salad leaves, a loaf of bread and some goat's cheese. Go home and make croûtons with golden, melted goat's cheese and a little walnut oil drizzled over the top. Serve with the fresh green salad and a glass of chilled white wine. Santé!

## *Salade de fromage de chèvre*
# GOAT'S CHEESE SALAD

*Preparation time: 20 minutes, plus making the vinaigrette*

1 head of yellow chicory

1 head of purple chicory

100g/3½oz rocket leaves

175g/6oz goat's cheese, such as Sainte Maure, Coeur de Lion La Buche or any other good-quality goat's cheese

20g/¾oz/¼ cup chopped walnuts or hazelnuts

1 recipe quantity French Vinaigrette (see page 20)

Cut off the base and outer leaves of the chicory, then cut each head into half, lengthways, and remove the core. Arrange the chicory and rocket on four plates, with the rocket in the middle. Crumble the goat's cheese over the salad and sprinkle with the walnuts. Drizzle with the dressing and serve.

CHEF'S TIP: *Add some hazelnut oil to your French Vinaigrette, making the dressing less classic but adding extra flavour to the salad. Also, to add extra crunch to your salad, toast the nuts in a frying pan over a medium heat, tossing them often and watching them closely so that they don't burn.*

## *Soufflé au fromage*

# CHEESE SOUFFLÉ

*Preparation time 40 minutes, plus chilling and infusing*
*Cooking time 45 minutes*

60g/2¼oz butter, softened

50g/1¾oz/heaped ⅓ cup plain flour

300ml/10½oz/scant 1¼ cups milk

1 bouquet garni, made with 1 parsley sprig, 1 thyme sprig and 1 small bay leaf, tied together with kitchen string

a pinch of freshly grated nutmeg

4 eggs, separated

100g/3½oz/¾ cup grated Cheddar cheese

100g/3½oz/¾ cup grated hard cheese, such as Comté, plus extra for sprinkling

cayenne pepper (or paprika for a milder flavour), for sprinkling

a few drops of lemon juice

60g/2¼oz mild, crumbly goat's cheese, diced

sea salt and freshly ground black pepper

Mix 50g/1¾oz of the butter with the flour until the mixture forms a smooth paste. Transfer to a small dish, cover with cling film and chill for 20 minutes.

Put the milk, bouquet garni and nutmeg in a small saucepan and bring to the boil over a high heat. Remove from the heat and set aside to infuse and cool down for about 15 minutes until warm.

Strain the milk mixture into a large saucepan and season with salt and pepper. Reheat gently over a medium-low heat to a simmer, then add the butter and flour paste bit by bit, stirring until the milk thickens. It should have a very smooth texture without any lumps. Continue to cook the milk mixture for a further 5 minutes, then add the egg yolks one by one, stirring until combined after each addition. Add 80g/2¾oz/⅔ cup each of the Cheddar and Comté cheeses and stir well. Season again with salt and pepper and set aside.

Grease four individual 9 x 5cm/3½ x 2in ramekins (or one round 18 x 8cm deep/7 x 3¼in deep soufflé dish) with the remaining butter, then coat the inside of the dishes with the remaining Cheddar and Comté cheeses, sprinkle a little cayenne pepper over and chill to set while you finish preparing the soufflé mixture.

Preheat the oven to 190°C/375°F/gas 5 and rub a large clean bowl with the lemon juice, then wipe dry. Put the egg whites in the bowl and beat with a whisk or electric mixer until medium to stiff peaks form. Avoid overbeating or the mixture will split and the soufflés will collapse. Whisk half the egg whites into the cheese mixture, then carefully fold in the rest, using a spatula, until smooth and firm but light.

Spoon half the mixture into the ramekin dishes, add the goat's cheese and then top with the remaining soufflé mixture. Smooth the tops and wipe the inside borders of the dishes clean with your thumb. Finally, sprinkle a little extra Comté over.

Bake the soufflés in the preheated oven for 10 minutes (12 minutes if you are making one large soufflé), then lower the temperature to 170°C/325°F/ gas 3 and bake for a further 15–20 minutes until well risen, golden brown and slightly trembling. Switch the oven off and leave the soufflés in the oven for a further 2–3 minutes, then remove from the oven. Serve immediately.

*Boeuf bourguignon*

*Foie de veau poêlé aux câpres, persil et cerfeuil*

*Steak au beurre d'herbes et citron*

*Boudin noir aux poires*

*Gigot d'agneau rôti à l'ail et lavande*

*Steak tartare*

*Cassoulet toulousain*

*Poulet au vin rouge*

## Les Viandes

# MEAT, POULTRY & GAME

There is such a diverse selection of meat and poultry from all around France that the possibilities are endless. In most brasseries you will find the traditional favourites, popular all over the country, as well as specialities from the individual region such as Roast Leg of Lamb with Garlic & Lavender in the south and classic Boeuf Bourguignon in Burgundy. Some of my personal favourites are from my own region. For me, you can't beat a farm-sourced Pork Steak with Mustard & Gherkin Sauce or Maman's Pot-Roasted Pheasant. This is real food – the food we love to eat. Eat to live or live to eat – no contest really!

There is so much you can do with the forgotten cuts of meat. Rump, oxtail, cheek and blade are good for a variety of uses, from minute steaks to stews, and they make a refreshing change from the classic fillet, sirloin or entrecôte. When growing up, we used to eat minute steaks and stews quite often. Maman always made them on Tuesdays, because that was market day and the meat was guaranteed to be fresh and of high quality. The classic minute steak is a terrific no-nonsense meal – great served with home-made fries and a seasonal salad or in a simple baguette with mustard.

*Steak au beurre d'herbes et citron*

# STEAK WITH HERB & LEMON BUTTER

*Preparation time 20 minutes, plus making the fries and salad*
*Cooking time 5 minutes*

2 tbsp sunflower oil

4 rump steaks, about 175g/6oz each, flattened

15g/½oz butter

sea salt and freshly ground black pepper

1 recipe quantity Large French Fries with Sea Salt (see page 165), to serve

seasonal salad, to serve

**LEMON & HERB BUTTER**

250g/9oz butter, softened

2 flat-leaf parsley sprigs, chopped

1 tarragon sprig, finely chopped

zest of 1 lemon

juice of ½ lemon

First, make the lemon and herb butter. Put the butter, herbs and lemon zest and juice in a bowl and season with salt and pepper. Mix together with a wooden spoon, then set aside 4 heaped teaspoons to use with the steaks.

Put a piece of cling film on a work surface and spoon half of the remaining lemon and herb butter along the middle. Wrap the cling film around the butter and roll into a log shape. Repeat with the remaining butter, then wrap each log in a piece of foil and freeze. You can then cut pieces off at your convenience for use on barbecues and grilled or pan-fried meats.

Now make the steaks. Warm the oil in a large, ridged griddle or frying pan over a medium heat. Season the steaks with salt and pepper and fry for 2 minutes. Just before turning them, add the plain butter. Turn and cook for a further 2 minutes. Try not to let the butter burn, as it would give the meat a burnt taste. It should be a lovely, light hazelnut colour.

Put your steaks, piping hot, on a plate and top each one with 1 teaspoon of the reserved lemon and herb butter. Let it melt into the steaks a little, then serve with large french fries and salad.

CHEF'S TIP: *To stop the edges of the steak from curling upwards when being cooked, use a small, sharp knife to 'nip' into the edges of the fat.*

This is an iconic French dish, and if you want to make it as the French do, you will probably use Charolais beef and a full-bodied Burgundy red wine. You don't need to use prime cuts of beef – the braising cuts, such as brisket, silverside, blade, cheek or even shank are more economical and give the dish much more flavour. In France, the process of cooking Boeuf Bourguignon often begins two days before serving, to soften up the meat and conserve the aromas – but a three-hour marinade will do just as well.

*Boeuf bourguignon*

# BEEF BOURGUIGNON

*Preparation time 20 minutes, plus
  3 hours marinating
Cooking time 2 hours 15 minutes*

800g/1lb 12oz beef brisket, cut into
  large cubes

1l/35fl oz/4 cups full-bodied red
  wine

2 thyme sprigs

4 garlic cloves, crushed with the flat
  edge of a knife or your hand

3 tbsp Cognac

100ml/3½fl oz/scant ½ cup
  sunflower oil

2 tbsp plain flour

600ml/21fl oz/scant 2½ cups veal
  stock or Chicken Stock
  (see page 18)

1 bouquet garni made with
  1 parsley sprig, 1 thyme sprig and
  1 small bay leaf, tied together with
  kitchen string

2 carrots, peeled, halved lengthways
  and cut into chunks

12 silverskin onions

100g/3½oz small button
  mushrooms

100g/3½oz pancetta, diced

1 handful of flat-leaf parsley, roughly
  chopped

salt and freshly ground pepper

1 recipe quantity Creamed Mashed
  Potatoes (see page 165), to serve

In a deep dish, mix together the beef, wine, thyme, garlic and Cognac. Cover with cling film and leave to marinate in the fridge for at least 3 hours.

Drain the meat into a bowl, using a colander, and reserve the marinade.

Heat 4 tablespoons of the oil in a large saucepan or cast iron pot over a medium heat. Add the meat and cook for 20 minutes until brown, season with salt and pepper, then sprinkle with the flour and cook, stirring, for a further 2–3 minutes. Add the stock and reserved marinade and bring to the boil. Skim the foam off the surface and add the bouquet garni, then reduce the heat to low and simmer, partially covered, for 1 hour 45 minutes, stirring occasionally, until the meat is tender. By that time you should have a rich, silky sauce.

About 50 minutes before the end of the cooking time, heat another medium saucepan with 1 tablespoon of the oil over a medium-low heat. Add the carrots and onions and cook for 10 minutes or until soft and pale gold in colour, then add to the meat saucepan.

When the beef is almost ready, heat the remaining oil in a frying pan over a medium heat. Add the mushrooms and pancetta and fry for 8–10 minutes, stirring occasionally, until golden brown, then add them to the beef. Check the seasoning adjusting the salt and pepper, if necessary, throw in the parsley and stir gently without breaking the delicate pieces of beef.

Serve hot with creamed mashed potatoes for a perfect winter warmer.

The classic Steak Tartare is made without tomato sauce or egg yolk, but it was traditionally served with tartare sauce, which is where its name comes from. This famous dish first appeared in French restaurants in the early 2oth century and has remained popular ever since. As it is made from raw beef, it is very important to use top-quality meat. If you use beef fillet, choose the end part of the fillet, and save the more expensive middle section for other uses. A cheaper cut I would recommend is sirloin, as it is as tender and tasty. Whichever cut you choose, make sure it is very fresh.

*Steak tartare*

# STEAK TARTARE

*Preparation time 20 minutes*

1 small shallot, finely chopped

1 tbsp chopped parsley leaves

1 tbsp Dijon mustard

1 tbsp tomato sauce

1 tbsp capers, chopped

2 egg yolks

2 tbsp olive oil

600g/1lb 5oz beef fillet or sirloin, trimmed of any sinew and cut into very small dice

sea salt and freshly ground black pepper

Mix the shallot, parsley, mustard, tomato sauce and capers in a medium-sized bowl. Add the egg yolks, season with salt and pepper, then drizzle in the olive oil while still mixing. Finally, stir in the beef and check and adjust the seasoning.

Divide the mixture into 4, shape into patties and serve.

CHEF'S TIP: *For a variation, I also like to make steak tartare using wasabi instead of mustard and a few drops of Worcestershire sauce.*

This dish is adored equally on both sides of the Channel. It is hard to find top-quality calves' liver, unless you know the farmer or your butcher has a good supplier, but it is well worth the search – calves' liver should be firm in texture and milky in colour. The success of your dish depends both on the quality of the liver and the way in which you cook it. Here it is simply pan-fried and served with a caper and herb butter, some delicious creamy mashed potatoes and warm, zesty buttered spinach. So easy to prepare, and really satisfying. I am a happy man.

*Foie de veau poêlé aux câpres, persil et cerfeuil*

# PAN-FRIED CALVES' LIVER WITH CAPERS, PARSLEY & CHERVIL

*Preparation time 15 minutes, plus making the potatoes and spinach*
*Cooking time 5 minutes*

4 calves' livers, about 150g/5½oz each and 1cm/½in thick

85g/3oz butter

2 tbsp rinsed chopped capers

1 small handful of flat-leaf parsley, chopped

1 small handful of chervil, chopped

sea salt and freshly ground black pepper

1 recipe quantity Creamed Mashed Potatoes (see page 165), to serve

1 recipe quantity Buttered Spinach with Lemon Zest (see page 162), to serve

Put the calves' liver on some kitchen towel and pat dry to ensure it fries rather than boils.

Warm half the butter in a large frying pan over a medium heat. When it is melted and a lovely golden colour, add the liver to the pan and cook for 2 minutes on each side or until medium-rare to medium and golden brown on both sides. Remove from the pan and keep warm.

Add the remaining butter to the pan, then add the capers, parsley and chervil, mixing with a wooden spoon. Season with salt and pepper, then pour the mixture over the liver. Serve hot with creamed mashed potatoes and buttered spinach with lemon zest.

It's funny the things that get us excited. For me it is the seasons – not just the colours and the smells, but knowing that soon certain produce is going to be available that hasn't been around for a while. When spring arrives, it is wild garlic first, then peas and, at last, the new season's spring lamb: milk-fed and unbelievably tender. Simply pan-roasted and served with courgettes, tomatoes and sauce vierge, this dish brings out all the freshness and colour of the Mediterranean. Enjoy it with a light rosé wine, close your eyes and there you are – in Provence.

*Agneau aux petits légumes et sauce vierge*

# ROAST LAMB WITH MEDITERRANEAN VEGETABLES & SAUCE VIERGE

*Preparation time 20 minutes, plus making the sauce*
*Cooking time 30 minutes*

2 lamb fillets or loin of lamb, fully trimmed

4 rosemary sprigs

2 tbsp olive oil

4 garlic cloves, unpeeled

salt and freshly ground black pepper

1 recipe quantity Sauce Vierge (see page 21), to serve

**MEDITERRANEAN VEGETABLES**

4–6 tbsp olive oil

2 plum tomatoes, cut into 5mm/¼in-thick rounds

2 small courgettes, cut into 5mm/¼in-thick rounds

1 aubergine, cut into 5mm/¼in-thick rounds

Preheat the oven to 220°C/425°F/gas 7. Season the lamb with salt and pepper, pierce each fillet on both sides with a sharp knife and insert a rosemary sprig into each opening. Heat an ovenproof frying pan over a medium heat and add the oil and garlic. Add the lamb and cook for about 5 minutes, turning continuously until sealed and golden brown all over, then put it in the oven for 5–8 minutes. Remove, set aside and keep warm.

Meanwhile, cook the vegetables. Heat a frying pan over a medium heat and add the oil. Add the vegetables in batches so they are in a single layer, season with salt and pepper and fry for 3–4 minutes on each side until just tender and golden.

Starting with the tomatoes, place 3 slices of tomato and 2 slices of courgette and aubergine, alternately and just overlapping, in the centre of each of four plates. Carve the lamb into thick slices on the diagonal and arrange on top of the vegetables. Spoon the Sauce Vierge over the lamb and on the plates and serve.

Why did I choose this dish? Simple – I love it! I think a lot of people feel the same way because it is delicious, easy to make and not too costly. The aromas that fill your kitchen are incredible, from the marinade right through to the roasting. Try to use herbs that are in season. In winter, use rosemary and thyme, for example, and in spring or summer, try *herbes de Provence*. If you are lucky enough to be able to pick fresh herbs, gently rub them in your hand before you throw them in the pot – this helps to release their essential oils. And don't forget to enjoy the fragrance left on your hand – it is a special moment where time stops for a few seconds, and you are glad to be exactly where you are.

*Jarrets d'agneau braisés au vin rouge*

# LAMB SHANKS BRAISED IN RED WINE

*Preparation time 20 minutes, plus making the stock, potatoes and ratatouille*
*Cooking time 2 hours 45 minutes*

4 small lamb shanks

2 tbsp sunflower oil

1 tbsp olive oil

1 onion, cut lengthways into 8 slices

2 carrots, peeled and chopped

1 celery stick, thinly sliced

2 tomatoes, quartered

1 garlic bulb, unpeeled and halved horizontally

750ml/26fl oz/3 cups full-bodied red wine

500ml/17fl oz/2 cups Lamb Stock (see page 18) or water

3 thyme or rosemary sprigs, or 1 small handful of mixed *herbes de Provence*

sea salt and freshly ground black pepper

1 recipe quantity Creamed Mashed Potatoes (see page 165), to serve

½ recipe quantity Ratatouille Provençale (see page 148), to serve

Put the lamb shanks on a plate, season well with salt and pepper, then rub the seasoning into the meat with your fingers. Heat the sunflower and olive oils in a cast iron pot over a medium to high heat. When the oils are hot but not burning, add the lamb shanks and cook, partially covered, for 20 minutes or until they turn a lovely golden brown colour. Make sure the heat is high enough to seal the meat, but not burn it, and turn frequently.

Add the onion, carrots, celery, tomatoes and garlic and cook, stirring frequently, for a further 10 minutes until the vegetables are a light golden colour. Add the wine, cover partially with a lid, and cook for 5 minutes or until the liquid has reduced by half. This reduction helps to remove the acidity from the wine.

Add the stock and bring to the boil over a high heat, then reduce the heat to low. Cover partially with a lid, leaving a very small gap, and simmer for 2 hours until the lamb is meltingly tender and the sauce has reduced down a little. Keep an eye on the pot during cooking. Turn the meat from time to time and make sure it doesn't braise too fast and dry out – you want to have some sauce at the end.

About half an hour before your lamb is ready, add the herbs and cover partially again. I can already smell the mix simmering in the pot and gently wafting around the kitchen – what a joy!

Serve hot with creamed mashed potatoes and ratatouille provençale.

CHEF'S TIP: *If by chance you find that you have used a wine that is too acidic and you don't realize it until you taste the dish, add 1 teaspoon caster sugar – this will help to rebalance the flavours.*

Rosemary and thyme are classic flavours to match with lamb, but lots of other herbs also go well with it. Personally, I find lavender wonderful. There are just two things to remember: measure it carefully (as too much can make your food bitter) and only use the flowers, not the stalks. A few years ago, while on holiday in Provence, we were walking to town to get some baguettes and *pains au chocolat* for breakfast when we found ourselves amid a sea of lavender fields. The colour and aroma were truly magical. On the way back we picked huge bunches of it. Some we tied together to take home and dry, and some I decided to put in the pot … this is what I made.

## *Gigot d'agneau rôti à l'ail et lavande*

# ROAST LEG OF LAMB WITH GARLIC & LAVENDER

*Preparation time 25 minutes, plus overnight marinating and making the potatoes*
*Cooking time 1 hour 10 minutes*

1.5kg/3lb 5oz leg of lamb

1 garlic bulb, unpeeled and halved horizontally

8 lavender sprigs, flower heads only

150ml/5fl oz/scant ⅔ cup olive oil

6 garlic cloves, peeled and halved

2 shallots, unpeeled and halved

sea salt and freshly ground black pepper

1 recipe quantity Sautéed Potatoes with Parsley & Garlic (see page 163), to serve

You need to prepare this dish the day before you want to eat it.

Put the lamb in a cling film-lined roasting tin that fits in the fridge and season with black pepper. (Don't season with salt now, as it draws the blood out of the lamb. Salt is always added just before cooking meat.) Add the garlic bulb and 6 heads of the lavender and pour 90ml/3fl oz/generous ⅓ cup of the oil over the top. Rub the seasonings in thoroughly, then wrap the lamb in the cling film and leave in the fridge overnight.

Preheat the oven to 200°C/400°F/gas 6. Unwrap the lamb, put it back in the roasting tin with the garlic bulb and dab it with kitchen towel. Pierce it several times with a sharp knife and push a halved garlic clove inside each opening. Add the shallots to the pan, pour the remaining oil over the top, season with salt and pepper and then roast in the preheated oven for 1 hour until golden brown on the outside but still pink and moist inside. Remove the lamb from the tin and wrap it in foil to keep warm.

Put 100ml/3½fl oz/scant ½ cup water in the roasting tin to deglaze, then return it to the oven and cook for 3–4 minutes until reduced. This will gather all the flavours from the caramelization of the meat and give you the concentrated juice you need.

Unwrap the lamb. You will find some juice has also gathered in the foil – add it to the juice in the roasting tin, stir and set aside.

Slice the lamb, then drizzle it with the juice, sprinkle with the remaining lavender flowers and serve with sautéed potatoes.

CHEF'S TIP: *While lavender is a stunning match with the lamb, this dish can be made with more traditional herbs, such as rosemary and thyme, or any other herbs of your choice, to create your personal twist.*

Sauerkraut (*choucroute* in French) became popular when the first brasserie was opened in Paris by a brewer from Alsace in northeastern France in the late 1800's. Today it can be found on most, if not all brasserie menus right across France, and in some brasseries it will be served up more than a hundred times a day. It is one of those traditional recipes, rarely written down and yet somehow passed on from generation to generation, and there is probably no greater statement of Alsatian identity with regard to food than *choucroute*. In this dish I team it with delicious smoked pork shoulder and sausages to make a superbly flavoursome combination.

*Choucroute alsacienne*

# SAUERKRAUT WITH PORK

*Preparation time 40 minutes*
*Cooking time 3 hours*

400g/14oz smoked pork shoulder or pancetta

80g/2¾oz duck fat

1 onion, chopped

1kg/2lb 4oz ready-made sauerkraut, drained, rinsed and gently pressed to remove any liquid

1 bouquet garni made with 1 small handful of parsley, 1 thyme sprig and 1 bay leaf, tied together with kitchen string

1 ready-made spice sachet or homemade with 4 juniper berries, 1 clove and a small pinch of cumin seeds, tied up in a small muslin cloth

200g/7oz pork belly

1l/35fl oz/4 cups bottled lager

1 tbsp vegetable bouillon powder

2 smoked German sausages, such as Strasbourg or Frankfurter

4 potatoes, peeled and cut in half

sea salt and freshly ground black pepper

mustard, to serve (optional)

Heat a heavy frying pan over a medium-high heat and cook the pork shoulder or pancetta and pork belly, turning continuously, for about 10 minutes until each piece has an even colour all around. Remove from the heat and set aside.

Heat the duck fat in a large saucepan over a medium heat. Add the onion and cook, covered, for 5 minutes, stirring occasionally until translucent but not coloured. Add the sauerkraut, bouquet garni, spice sachet, sealed pork shoulder and belly, lager and bouillon powder, then cover and cook gently for 1½ hours over a medium-low heat. Check regularly and stir occasionally so the ingredients do not burn and stick to the bottom of the pan.

Remove the lid from the saucepan, add the sausages and cook, covered, for a further 30 minutes. Add the potatoes, then cook for a further 20 minutes until the potatoes are tender, making sure there is still a bit of liquid in the pan. If the liquid is too low, add 250ml/9fl oz/1 cup water.

Remove from the heat and take out the bouquet garni and spice sachet. Season with salt and pepper, then transfer the sauerkraut to a large serving dish. Cut the meat, sausages and potatoes and serve on top of the sauerkraut. You can also have some mustard on the side, which is especially delicious with the sausages.

I love pork and the moisture and flavour of its delicate fat. If you buy it trimmed of fat, you buy it trimmed of flavour! The meat also dries out and loses its goodness. Animals raised as free-range have a far more varied diet, which makes their meat deliciously succulent – perhaps we notice the improvement in succulence with free-range pigs more because they are bred to be fatter than other animals. For me, the fattier cuts, such as pork belly, are best roasted first and then braised long and slow. I promise, they are well worth the wait.

*Poitrine de porc confite aux pommes*

# PORK BELLY CONFIT WITH APPLES

*Preparation time 25 minutes, plus overnight marinating and making the cabbage and potatoes*
*Cooking time 4 hours 30 minutes*

juice of 1 lemon

1kg/2lb 4oz apples

1.25kg/2lb 12oz skinless, boneless pork belly, fat layer on

90ml/3fl oz/generous ⅓ cup sunflower oil

15g/½oz butter

1 recipe quantity Braised Cabbage, (see page 158), to serve

1 recipe quantity Fondant Potatoes with Confit of Garlic (see page 164), to serve

**MARINADE**

3 carrots, peeled and halved lengthways

3 onions, quartered

4 thyme sprigs

1 cinnamon stick, halved

1 star anise, halved

4 tbsp sea salt

1.2l/40fl oz/4¾ cups cider

freshly ground black pepper

First, put the lemon juice in a bowl of water and set aside. Peel the apples, reserving the skins for the marinade, and dip the fruit in the lemon water to prevent oxidization. Wrap the apples in kitchen towel, then place in a dish, cover with cling film and set aside in the fridge.

In another bowl, mix together the reserved apple skins and all the marinade ingredients, except the cider. Put half of this mixture in a large baking tray lined with kitchen foil. Put the pork belly on top, then cover with the remaining marinade mixture. Pour the cider over, cover with a sheet of greaseproof paper and leave to marinate in the fridge overnight.

Preheat the oven to 140°C/275°F/gas 1. Remove the pork from the marinade and dry it on a clean tea towel. Warm the sunflower oil in a large frying pan over a medium heat and cook the pork for about 18–20 minutes, turning occasionally, until golden brown but not crispy or burnt.

Meanwhile, transfer the marinade to a saucepan, bring it to the boil over a high heat and skim it with a slotted spoon to remove any foam that rises to the surface. Return the pork to the baking tray and pour the marinade over. Cover with greaseproof paper to prevent the top from drying and bake for 4 hours or until the meat is very soft. You can check this by sliding a pointed knife through the meat.

When the pork is almost ready, cut each peeled apple into 4 or 6 wedges. Melt the butter in a frying pan over a medium heat and sauté the apples for 6–8 minutes or until golden brown.

Transfer the meat to a wooden board, cut into portions and serve warm with the apples, braised cabbage and fondant potatoes.

CHEF'S TIP: *If you have any leftover pork, cover it with greaseproof paper and keep refrigerated. Serve the following day as a cold meat starter with pickles, mustard and farm bread.*

If you are concerned about the fat content of cuts such as pork belly, pork collar steak is a delicious, lower-fat alternative. One of the things I love about pork is how versatile it is. It can accommodate so many flavours, so many different spices and be cooked in so many ways: grilled, roasted, stir-fried or stewed. It can even be served cold with mustard on baguette. Its succulence and flavour make it perfect every time. It is always important to balance dishes well, which is why I like this one so much – the richness of the cream and pork are offset beautifully by the sharpness of the gherkin and mustard sauce.

*Côtes de porc, sauce moutarde et cornichons*

# PORK STEAKS WITH MUSTARD & GHERKIN SAUCE

*Preparation time 10 minutes, plus making the potatoes*
*Cooking time 15 minutes*

2 tbsp sunflower oil

4 pork collar steaks, about 150g/ 5½ oz each

30g/1oz butter

80ml/2½fl oz/⅓ cup single cream

1 tsp wholegrain mustard

1 tarragon sprig

4 small gherkins, halved and sliced into strips

sea salt and freshly ground black pepper

1 recipe quantity Creamed Mashed Potatoes (see page 165), to serve

Preheat the oven to 140°C/275°F/gas 1. Warm the oil in a non-stick frying pan over a medium heat. Add the steaks and cook for 3–4 minutes on each side until golden brown, adding the butter when you turn them over. Remove from the pan and keep warm in the oven.

Add 4 tablespoons water to the pan to deglaze. You should end up with a pale golden liquid. Bring to a simmer over a low heat and slowly stir in the cream and mustard. Add the tarragon and gherkins and season with salt and pepper.

Divide the steaks onto four plates, pour the sauce over and serve immediately with creamed mashed potatoes – perfect for soaking up the sauce.

Originating from Castelnaudary in the 14th century, cassoulet is a gorgeous, satisfying, slowly simmered casserole. It is one of the best-known French dishes worldwide and is probably as near as you will get to a French National Dish. Haricot beans are at the heart of it, with the addition of meat or poultry of some kind, although never chicken or fish. In some cities it is made with pork, in others with mutton, goose or duck and, during the shooting season, game birds are also used. By the way, the name 'cassoulet' comes from the word 'cassole', a glazed earthenware pot specially designed for this dish.

*Cassoulet toulousain*

# TOULOUSE CASSOULET

*Preparation time 25 minutes, plus soaking the beans*
*Cooking time 5 hours 15 minutes*

300g/10½oz/1½ cups dried white haricot beans

1 clove

2 onions, 1 peeled and left whole and 1 chopped

100g/3½oz pork rind

300g/10½oz pork belly, skin removed, or pork shoulder

4 garlic cloves

4 tbsp duck fat

400g/14oz pork collar

2 carrots, peeled and chopped

1 bouquet garni made with 1 parsley sprig, 1 thyme sprig and 1 bay leaf, tied together with kitchen string

4 tbsp tomato purée

4 Toulouse sausages

85g/3oz/1 cup fresh white breadcrumbs

sea salt and freshly ground pepper

Put the beans in a bowl, cover with water and leave to soak for 20 minutes. Meanwhile, insert the clove into the whole onion and set aside.

Rinse the beans in cold water and drain, then transfer to a large flameproof casserole dish. Add the clove-stuffed onion, pork rind, pork belly and garlic, then add enough water to cover all the ingredients completely. Partially cover the casserole and place over a medium heat. Bring to a very gentle simmer, reduce the heat to low and simmer for up to 2½ hours until the meat is tender and the beans are cooked but still slightly firm. When the beans are ready, season with salt and pepper and remove from the heat. Set aside, uncovered.

Meanwhile, after the bean mixture has been cooking for 2 hours, heat the duck fat in a large earthenware dish or large, deep saucepan over a medium heat. Add the pork collar and cook for 8–10 minutes until golden brown, then add the chopped onion, carrots and bouquet garni. Add about half of the liquid from the bean mixture, then top up with enough water to cover all the ingredients completely. Stir in the tomato purée. Cover and place over a medium-low heat and cook at a gentle simmer for 2 hours, or until the pork is very tender, then add the sausages and cook for a further 30 minutes.

Preheat the oven to 180°C/350°F/gas 4. Remove the pork collar and sausages from the earthenware dish and put them in a large baking dish. Discard the bouquet garni. Pour the bean mixture and remaining contents from the pork collar dish over them and sprinkle with the breadcrumbs. Bake for 30 minutes in the preheated oven until the sauce has thickened slightly and the top is golden brown.

The sausage-making tradition in France has lasted well over 2,000 years and black pudding, *boudin noir,* is one of the oldest charcuterie preparations. It is very perishable and so is produced on a daily basis in French charcuteries, and it should be used on the day you buy it. Each charcuterie will make it in a slightly different way from the other: different seasonings, fruit and vegetables will be used and some may add chestnuts and various aromatic ingredients. However they do it, it is incredibly popular both in brasseries and at home. I sometimes like to serve it with apples or quince, but I particularly enjoy it with pear as I have done here.

*Boudin noir aux poires*

# BLACK PUDDING WITH PEARS

*Preparation time 20 minutes*
*Cooking time 25 minutes*

600g/1lb 5oz black pudding

20g/¾oz butter

2 large pears, peeled, cored and
    cut into 16 wedges

1 shallot, finely sliced

1 tbsp brown sugar

2 tbsp reduced balsamic vinegar

1 tbsp sunflower oil

Bring a saucepan of salted water to the boil over a medium heat, then add the black pudding and simmer for 2–3 minutes. Remove from the heat and set aside. It is not imperative that you prepare the black pudding in this way, but it will help prevent it from splitting open.

Melt the butter in a medium frying pan over a medium heat. Add the pears and cook for 3–4 minutes until a pale, golden brown. Add the shallot and cook for about 4 minutes until softened, then add the sugar, balsamic vinegar and 3 tablespoons water. Cook for 2–3 minutes until the mixture has the consistency of a runny syrup. The pear wedges should still retain their shape and not be too soft. Remove from the heat and set aside.

Slice the black pudding into approximately 5mm/¼in-thick rounds. Heat the sunflower oil in another medium-sized frying pan over a low heat. Add the black pudding and cook for 6–8 minutes until browned on both sides and warmed through. You do not want to cook it too fast or it will burst.

To serve, divide the shallot mix from the pan with the pears onto four plates. Arrange the black pudding on the plates and then the pears. Spoon any remaining syrup over.

# *La Charcuterie*

# *Charcuterie*

The word *charcuterie* originated from the French term *chair cuite* – 'cooked meat'. Today, it has come to mean the art and science of the pig – in other words, the butchering, fabrication and preparation of pork – but it is also a term used more generally for all sorts of cold meat, poultry and fish products and dishes.

At home, we often had charcuterie of cold meat with fresh baguette, gherkins and radishes. This was our usual starter in spring and summer, and we loved it. Then came the main course, which may have been smoked pork shoulder, roasted and then braised with cabbage or turnip. In Lure, my hometown, every Tuesday was market day, when the large town square was filled with local producers selling livestock. You could choose your pig, hen, duck, turkey, rabbit and a lot more for your dinner or for your farm. Once a month, farmers from all over the county would come to the market to meet, make deals and buy livestock. I used to walk among them and listen to the stories they told. Sometimes, big arguments would break out, and in the regional dialect too, which was so hard to understand. There was never a dull moment.

My family always bought from the same *charcutier*. Maman and Papa liked his products, and as he came from near Maman's village, he was almost a friend. He always reserved stuff for us and gave us something extra to eat and try, whether it was salami, or a speciality such as *cervelas* (a cooked sausage from Alsace, often served in salad or simply grilled) which was full of garlic but so good. Several years later, when I was starting my apprenticeship at a hotel in the town of Luxeuil-les-Bains, I learned how to make a few of the charcuterie products I used to eat. Maman's and Papa's *charcutier* supplied the hotel. The hotel and the *chef patron* had a tremendous reputation in the region and everything was home-made. During my training I often had to prep the fowls, rabbit, deer or other animals before I started to make a dish. It wasn't easy, but I was learning – after all, that was why I was there.

One of the most important charcuterie dishes I learned to make was terrines: a mixture of meat, fish, poultry or seafood, packed into rectangular dishes and often cooked in a bain-marie. Usually served in the container in which they are made and accompanied by pickles or even a sauce, they formed part of a buffet display. Another form of charcuterie I learned how to make was pâté, often *en croûte* (in pastry). This is a rich meat, game or fish mixture baked in a pastry crust (usually puff pastry), which can be served hot or cold as a starter, as part of a cold buffet or as a meal in itself. Today there is an abundance of different pâtés to choose from, with ingredients including chestnuts, red wine, herbs and spices. Other important charcuterie dishes in my region were *rillettes*: a preparation of pork, rabbit, goose or duck meat chopped, salted, cooked in goose fat and then pounded to a paste and potted (great on toast!); and *boudin noir*, or black pudding, a savoury sausage consisting largely of pork blood and fat, seasoned and contained in intestine, which forms the skin. Butchers in France all have their own recipes for this, which vary from adding onion and seasoning to including fruit, vegetables, herbs, cream, semolina, breadcrumbs, and so on. In my region, they add milk and onions. *Boudin noir* is delicious fried with apples and served with mashed potatoes.

I was lucky to have such rigorous training and thankfully many artisan producers are going back to the basics – and people love it. In the Vosges area there are now plenty of *fermes-auberges*, farmhouse inns, which rear their own animals and grow their own produce to sell in their shops and to use in their kitchens.

Such shops are always full and they offer great value for money. Word of mouth brings people from all over to sample their products. Charcuterie features heavily, of course, and here you can find and enjoy all the regional specialities, from *Rosette de Lyon* salami (an exquisite, cured *saucisson* made from finely minced pork from animals that live on a pure vegetarian diet) to *Saucisse de Toulouse* (a traditional sausage from Toulouse made of coarsely diced pork and flavoured with wine, garlic and seasoning). It tastes great in cassoulet. I should also give a special mention to foie gras terrine, which is very popular during the festive season in France. A rare delicacy for food lovers, but a sensitive subject in general, it is made with goose or duck livers.

No discussion of charcuterie would be complete without mentioning *pancetta*, the cured, spiced pork belly that adds so much flavour to many recipes, and the many delicious types of ham there are to enjoy. There is *jambon cuit* (classic cooked ham), which is baked very slowly overnight in a low oven and traditionally kept in its brine for a few weeks, as well as tender *jambon cru* (uncooked ham), such as *Jambon de Luxeuil*. Similar to Bayonne ham, this is pickled in brine, dried, sometimes smoked and matured for a month before being used.

Charcuterie products are the ideal foods for eating with family and friends. There is a huge range of regional specialities to explore and enjoy, many of which have found their way onto brasserie menus. I have included my favourites in this book and invite you to share them. *Bon appétit!*

## A BRIEF HISTORY OF CHARCUTERIE

An ancient art that commenced nearly 6,000 years ago, charcuterie became popular during the Roman Empire when food started to become sophisticated. Since then, it has spread to many countries with diverse traditions and myriad culinary methods.

Charcuterie was extremely popular in France during the Middle Ages, when the country acquired many varieties of meatloaves, sausages and other meat products that were prepared and sold in specialist shops known as *charcuteries*, owned and run by *charcutiers*, who needed the talent to season and cook delicious food and present it well to attract customers. They experimented with different meats and game, resulting in new foods for their customers. This created a lot of competition between the *charcutiers*. The popular products and processes spread from France to neighbouring regions, including Germany. Frankfurt in Germany became famous for the 'Frankfurter', a smoked sausage that evolved into the American hot dog, while Genoa in Italy became renowned for its salami.

Now, more than 500 years later, you still find such foods in local or regional supermarkets. Stop at a motorway restaurant or shop in France and you are likely to find charcuterie in all its forms, from packaged goods to freshly made products, ready to buy and consume on the spot. If you happen to cross France from north to south or east to west, you will be able to learn a lot about each region simply by paying attention to what is on offer to eat at that time of year. Like cheeses and regional recipes, the range of charcuterie is vast, but each region claims the authenticity of their dishes or specialities. My region, Franche-Comté, is bordered by Alsace, the Vosges, Jura, Burgundy and Germany, so there are dozens of specialities. One of the best known is *saucisse de Morteau* from Morteau in Doubs, a smoked sausage made from a mixture of minced, seasoned meats. Traditionally, it is smoked in Tuyé chimneys, found in houses typical of the region. This sausage is cooked in boiling water or braised before you eat it and is delicious with lentils. Other specialities include *jambon fumé*, smoked ham, in Luxeuil-les-Bains and *palette fumée*, tripe sausage, from the Vosges region. Luckily, all of these regional foods have entered the world of the brasserie, so you can enjoy them almost anywhere in France.

LEFT PAGE CLOCKWISE FROM TOP LEFT:
jambon de Bayonne, bûchettes de saucisson,
saucisson de Bigorre, lomo, saucisse au
piment

RIGHT PAGE CLOCKWISE FROM TOP
LEFT: boudin noir (black pudding), salami,
chorizo, terrine de porc, coppa des Pyrénées,
ventrèche (pancetta), magret de canard fumé
(smoked duck breast)

This dish is a variation on Coq au Vin, which is such a classic that it can be found in almost every brasserie in every region of France. The difference between one Coq au Vin and another is very subtle: the wine used will most likely be one from that region, and some cooks use more heavily smoked bacon than others. But, it is generally agreed that you can't improve on perfection, so no one tries. Coq au Vin has mushrooms in it and silverskin onions rather than shallots, so my dish is called a casserole, not a coq au vin.

*Poulet au vin rouge*

# CHICKEN CASSEROLE IN RED WINE

*Preparation time 20 minutes, plus making the stock and cooking the tagliatelle*
*Cooking time 1 hour 15 minutes*

2–3 tbsp flour, for dusting

1 large chicken, about 1.5kg/ 3lb 5oz, cut into 8 pieces

1 tbsp sunflower oil

1 shallot, chopped

30g/1oz pancetta

2 large carrots, peeled and sliced

2 garlic cloves, unpeeled and crushed with the flat edge of a knife or your hand

350ml/12fl oz/scant 1½ cups Burgundy red wine, or your choice of regional red table wine

600ml/21fl oz/scant 2½ cups Chicken Stock (see page 18)

55g/2oz butter, diced

1 handful of tarragon, leaves only, or 3–4 thyme sprigs

sea salt and freshly ground black pepper

tagliatelle, cooked, to serve (optional)

Sprinkle the flour into a flat dish, season with salt and pepper and toss the chicken through the flour until it is lightly coated, then set aside. (The flour will help the sauce thicken while it's cooking.) Heat the oil in a cast iron or heavy-based casserole dish over a medium heat. Add the shallot, pancetta, carrots and garlic and cook for 5 minutes until softened but not coloured, then remove from the pan and set aside.

Put the chicken in the casserole dish and cook over a medium heat for 8–10 minutes, turning as necessary, until it has an even colour all around. Add the wine and cook for 10–12 minutes or until reduced by half. Add the stock and the shallot mixture and bring to the boil over a high heat. Skim the surface to remove any fat, then reduce the heat to low and cook, partially covered, for 15–20 minutes.

Remove the chicken from the casserole dish and set aside. Heat the cooking liquid, uncovered, over a medium heat for about 12–15 minutes until it reduces and turns into a lovely, light shiny syrup. Remove from the heat and stir in the butter until melted and combined. Put the chicken back in the dish and add the tarragon, keeping aside a few sprigs to sprinkle on top. Serve immediately with fresh tagliatelle, if liked.

*Blanc de poulet au ragoût de petits légumes et lardons*

# PAN-FRIED CHICKEN WITH GARDEN VEGETABLE & PANCETTA RAGOÛT

*Preparation time 20 minutes, plus making the stock*
*Cooking time 1 hour*

1.5kg/3lb 5oz broad beans in the pods and then shelled, or 400g/14oz/heaped 2 cups shelled broad beans

2 tbsp sunflower oil

4 chicken breasts on the bone, about 180g/6¼oz each

60g/2¼oz butter

2 garlic cloves, unpeeled and crushed with the flat edge of a knife or your hand

1 small handful of summer savory (*sarriette*) or 2 thyme sprigs

14 spring onions, white bulb only and root cut off

a pinch of caster sugar

100g/3½oz pancetta, diced

1 tsp thyme leaves

4 tbsp Chicken Stock (see page 18) or water

sea salt and freshly ground black pepper

Bring a saucepan of lightly salted water to the boil. Add the broad beans and blanch for 20 seconds, then drain and refresh immediately in a bowl of ice-cold water and drain again. Peel the beans and discard the outer skins. I know it's a fiddly job, but it's worth the trouble as it changes the flavour completely. Set aside for your ragoût.

Warm the oil in a large heavy-based frying pan or cast iron pan over a medium heat. Season the chicken with salt and pepper and cook, skin-side down and partially covered, for 8 minutes or until golden brown and slightly crispy. Turn the chicken over and add a knob of the butter along with the garlic and summer savory sprigs. Reduce the heat to low and cook for a further 8 minutes. Transfer to a serving dish, cover with kitchen foil and keep warm. Set the pan aside for making the jus later.

To make the ragoût, melt a knob of the remaining butter in a small frying pan over a medium heat. Add the spring onions and cook, stirring frequently, for 5–6 minutes until light golden. Season with salt and pepper and sprinkle in the sugar. Add 4 tablespoons water and cook over a low heat, partially covered, for 12–15 minutes or until the water has almost evaporated and the spring onions are slightly glazed.

Meanwhile, bring a saucepan of water to the boil. Add the pancetta and blanch for 1–2 minutes, then drain, refresh immediately in a bowl of cold water and drain again. Don't be tempted to blanch the pancetta any longer or it will turn too dry. Pat dry with kitchen towel.

Sauté the pancetta in a medium frying pan over a medium heat for about 4 minutes until slightly crispy. Stir in the broad beans, spring onions and thyme leaves and keep warm.

To make the jus, add the stock to the pan you roasted the chicken in and simmer for 2 minutes over a medium-low heat, then add the juices that will have collected under your chicken and stir in the remaining butter to give it a velvety shine.

Remove the chicken breasts from the bone, cut each of the 4 breasts into thick slices and arrange on a plate. Divide the ragoût onto the four plates, spoon the jus over and serve.

*Poule au pot, sauce gribiche*

# POACHED CHICKEN WITH SAUCE GRIBICHE

*Preparation time 1 hour*
*Cooking time 1 hour 25 minutes*

1 large chicken, about
   1.5–1.8kg/3lb 5oz–4lb

1 tarragon sprig

1 bouquet garni made with
   2 parsley sprigs, 1 thyme sprig and
   1 small bay leaf, tied together with
   kitchen string

1 celery stick, peeled and cut in half

4 large carrots, peeled and cut in
   half lengthways

2 leeks, washed, cut in half
   lengthways and tied together

2 small turnips, peeled and cut in
   half

1 small cabbage, cut into quarters

4 cloves

2 small onions, cut in half

sea salt and freshly ground black
   pepper

bread, to serve

**SAUCE GRIBICHE**

1 tsp white wine vinegar, plus
   1 tsp for hard-boiling the eggs

4 eggs

1 tsp of Dijon mustard

250ml/9fl oz/1 cup sunflower oil
   or light olive oil

40g/1½oz/¼ cup chopped gherkins

40g/1½oz/¼ cup capers, chopped

1 flat-leaf parsley sprig, leaves only,
   finely chopped

1 tarragon sprig, leaves only, finely
   chopped

1 chervil sprig, leaves only, finely
   chopped

Put the chicken in a large saucepan, season with a handful of sea salt and cover with water. Bring to the boil over a high heat, then skim the foam that rises to the top, using a ladle. Reduce the heat so that the chicken is only simmering, then add the tarragon, bouquet garni, celery, carrots, leeks, turnips and cabbage. Push a clove into each of the onion halves and add to the saucepan. Cook the chicken for 1¼ hours until the meat is very tender and falling off the bone.

Meanwhile, make the sauce gribiche. Fill a small saucepan with water and bring to the boil. Add a teaspoon of vinegar to the water, as this will make the eggs easier to shell after cooking. Place 1 egg in a ladle, then slowly and carefully slide the egg into the water so that you don't break the shell. Repeat for the remaining 3 eggs. Cook for 8 to 9 minutes until hard-boiled, drain and place the eggs under running cold water. When cool enough to handle, shell the eggs and cut in half.

Using a pestle and mortar or a food processor, mash the hard-boiled egg yolks until they form a smooth paste. Mix in the mustard and season with salt and pepper. While still mixing, add the vinegar, then slowly add the oil until the consistency resembles mayonnaise. Fold the gherkins, capers and herbs into the mixture and adjust the salt and pepper, if necessary. Finely chop the cooked egg whites and add them to the sauce. If you like, this sauce can be made the night before and chilled in the fridge.

Now it is time to enjoy. Serve the broth as a first course with a piece of bread – it is really good – then remove the chicken from the pan and cut it into pieces. Serve with the vegetables and Sauce Gribiche.

CHEF'S TIP: *You can replace the chicken with a piece of braising beef or even pork. For the best results, I would recommend blade, top side or silverside for the beef and, for the pork, the belly or collar. And if you like marrow, even better. It's great for serving with the beef.*

This is another very French salad found on every brasserie menu. It is very refreshing, with a nice crunch. You can use chervil instead of the tarragon; it is a wonderful herb that should be grown and used more often! Another delicious alternative is to use Saffron Mayonnaise (see page 21) instead of garlic mayonnaise and flat-leaf parsley instead of tarragon.

*Salade de blancs de volaille grillés*

# CHARGRILLED CHICKEN SALAD

*Preparation time 35 minutes, plus
20 minutes marinating
Cooking time 15 minutes*

4 chicken breasts, skin on

olive oil, for seasoning

1 tsp vinegar

8 quail eggs

2 tbsp garlic mayonnaise

2 tbsp chopped tarragon

juice of 1 small lemon

1 cos lettuce, cut into large pieces

2 tbsp croûtons

sea salt and freshly ground black pepper

Put the chicken breasts in a small dish, season with salt and pepper and drizzle with olive oil. Cover with cling film and leave to marinate for 15–20 minutes.

Meanwhile, soft-boil the quail eggs. Fill a small saucepan with water and bring to the boil. Add the vinegar to the water, as this will make the eggs easier to shell after cooking. Place the eggs in a ladle, then slowly and carefully slide them into the water so that you don't break the shells. Cook for 4 minutes, drain and place the eggs under running cold water. When cool enough to handle, shell the eggs, cut in half and set aside.

Preheat the oven to 200°C/400°F/gas 6. Heat a ridged griddle pan over a medium heat and fry the chicken breasts, skin-side down, for 5 minutes, then turn them over and fry for another 5 minutes. Your chicken breasts should now have charred grill marks on both sides. Transfer to a baking dish and roast in the preheated oven for a further 10 minutes.

Meanwhile, put the mayonnaise, tarragon and lemon juice in a large serving bowl, season with salt and pepper and mix well. Add the lettuce and mix.

Remove the chicken from the oven and cut it into thick slices while it is still warm. Arrange the slices on top of the salad and top with the quail eggs and finally the croûtons. Serve warm.

It was Grand-Mère Suzanne who taught me how to make food for the chickens on the farm – cooked jacket potatoes, still warm, crushed together with grain and water by hand. I can still remember how sore my hands would get after a while. Once made, we would put the mix in the tray and call the chickens by shouting "*piu, piu, piu*". They would all charge over, clucking in anticipation. When the chickens had devoured the mix, we would throw them some corn, too. All this was done twice a day – now that's the way to treat chickens! We fed them well knowing that one day they were going to feed us, and when it was time to put them in the pot we didn't feel too sad, as we knew it was just nature taking its course. This is a very traditional recipe, normally prepared with baby chicken called *poussin*, however, you could also use guinea fowl for a change – an often forgotten poultry that is quite delicious. Here I've used one larger chicken to serve four.

*Poulet fermier à la crapaudine*
# SPATCHCOCKED CHICKEN

*Preparation time 30 minutes*
*Cooking time 50 minutes*

1 x 1.25kg/2lb 12oz chicken, cut in half along both sides of the back bone, but kept as a whole piece

2 tbsp olive oil

100g/3½oz butter, melted

Dijon mustard or wasabi paste, for brushing (optional)

100g/3½oz/1 cup fresh breadcrumbs

sea salt and freshly ground black pepper

chilli-flavoured olive oil, to serve

Preheat the oven to 200°C/400°F/gas 6. Place the chicken on a chopping board, breast bone facing down, and press down firmly with the heels of your hands to break the joints and flatten. Season with salt and pepper and brush with the olive oil and 30g/1oz of the melted butter. Place skin-side up in a baking tray in the oven and roast for 35–40 minutes.

Remove from the oven and preheat the grill to low. Drizzle the chicken evenly with the remaining melted butter, then brush with the mustard or wasabi, if using, and cover with the breadcrumbs. Place under the grill and cook gently for a further 10 minutes, checking often to make sure the breadcrumbs don't burn. Cut the chicken into 4 and serve immediately with a chilli oil dressing.

This is a great brasserie dish from the south west of France, the foie gras region. There are so many varieties of duck to choose from: Gressingham, Mallard, Canard Croisé, but for this dish I recommend Barbary Duck, corn-fed if possible, but definitely free range. For me this is hearty winter food, which is not to say that it is too heavy for the summer: served with salad it can make a terrific outdoor lunch. Whatever the season, you can't beat the flavour of crispy duck legs.

*Confit de canard aux lentilles*

# DUCK CONFIT WITH LENTILS

*Preparation time 40 minutes, plus making the vinaigrette and 6–8 hours marinating*
*Cooking time 3–4 hours*

### CONFIT

4 duck legs, about 175g/6oz each, including fat

40g/1½oz sea salt

4 garlic cloves, unpeeled and crushed with the flat edge of a knife or your hand

4 thyme sprigs, leaves only

1kg/2lb 4oz goose or duck fat, melted

2 tbsp honey

freshly ground black pepper

### LENTILS

200g/7oz/1 cup Puy lentils, picked over and rinsed

1 shallot

1 small carrot, peeled and diced

1 bouquet garni made with 1 thyme sprig and 1 parsley sprig, tied together with kitchen string

1 garlic clove, unpeeled

2–3 tablespoons French Vinaigrette (see page 20)

1 handful of chervil, leaves only, chopped

To make the duck leg confit, put the duck legs in a small baking tray, skin-side down. Season with salt, pepper, garlic and thyme, cover with cling film, press down and leave to marinate for 2–3 hours in the fridge.

Preheat the oven to 130°C/250°F/gas 1. Take the duck out of the tray discarding the marinade, rinse under running cold water and dry on kitchen towel. Put the duck in a large heavy-based casserole or cast iron pan and pour the melted goose fat on top. Cover with a lid or greaseproof paper sealed with foil, place in the preheated oven and bake for 3–4 hours. Remove from the oven, skim off any fat, cover with foil and set aside. Alternatively, you can gently simmer the duck on the stove, covered, for 3–4 hours.

Meanwhile, make the lentils. Put them in a small saucepan and cover with cold water. Bring to the boil and skim the white foam from the surface. Add the shallot, carrot, bouquet garni and garlic, reduce the heat to low and simmer for a further 10 minutes or until al dente. Strain, reserving 2 tablespoons of the cooking liquid, and discard the shallot, bouquet garni and garlic, but leave the carrots in. Add the vinaigrette, the reserved cooking liquid and the chervil. Taste and adjust the seasoning with salt and pepper. This should give you a lovely salad.

Finally, brush the duck legs with the honey and pan-roast them skin-side down in a non-stick pan over a medium heat for 5 minutes or until crispy and golden brown. The honey will caramelize very quickly, so be careful not to let it burn.

Divide the lentils onto four plates, arrange the duck legs on top and enjoy! Alternatively, arrange in a large pot to serve from at the table. The texture and delicate flavours of this dish are second to none.

Les Trois-Épis is a high plateau on the Alsatian side of the Vosges mountains near Turckheim – it is surrounded by sweeping vineyards and has a stunning view of the valley below. Best known for the great Alsace wine it produces, it is also a hunting estate and became one of the favourite stomping grounds for my father and I whenever the hunting season arrived each year. A lesser known fact about Les Trois-Épis is that there are an unbelievable number of pheasants hiding among the vineyards eating grapes. When we started plucking pheasants at home as children, what struck us most was the colour of the flesh – it was deep purple and smelt strongly of wine! The flavour was already so tremendous that my mother didn't need much more than a few pieces of pancetta and some shallots to finish it off! She always preferred to roast pheasants in the pot, partly to retain the moisture, but also, I think, because she loved to lift the lid and smell the beautiful aroma. I can taste it like it was yesterday! Ah … those are the days I miss!

*Faisan façon Maman*

# MAMAN'S POT-ROASTED PHEASANT

*Preparation time 20–25 minutes, plus making the braised cabbage*
*Cooking time 1 hour 20 minutes*

1 young pheasant, prepared by your butcher (including liver chopped and returned to the cavity)

2 slices of pancetta or smoked bacon

4 tbsp sunflower oil

60g/2¼oz butter

2 apples, peeled, cored and quartered

1 bouquet garni made with 1 thyme sprig and 1 parsley sprig, tied together with kitchen string

2 tbsp brandy

250ml/9fl oz/1 cup double cream

sea salt and freshly ground black pepper

1 recipe quantity Braised Cabbage (see page 158) or vegetables of your choice, to serve

Take the pheasant, wrap the pancetta slices around the breast and tie it all up with kitchen string – this will hold everything together, keeping the pheasant breast moist.

Heat 2 tablespoons of the oil and the butter in a cast iron pot over a medium heat, then add the pheasant and pot roast, partially covered, for 40–45 minutes until the meat is well sealed and almost cooked through. Turn the pheasant occasionally to make sure you get an even rich golden colour all around.

Reduce the heat to low and add the apples, bouquet garni and brandy. With a wooden spoon, stir the ingredients to lift any tasty bits that have stuck to the base of the saucepan. Partially cover and cook for a further 10 minutes, then add the cream and simmer gently, uncovered, for a further 25 minutes or until the sauce is thick enough to coat the back of a spoon. Season with salt and pepper.

Serve the pheasant topped with the sauce and accompanied with braised cabbage or other vegetables of your choice.

In France, when we have the combination of truffles and potatoes in a dish, we talk about the rich mixing with the poor! Truffles can be expensive, but you don't need much and the addition can transform the simple into the spectacular. You can also freeze them if you have any left over. For this dish you can use chicken, but I find guinea fowl has so much more texture and flavour. Originally a wild bird, it has since been farmed – which I am glad about, otherwise people would really have missed out.

*Blancs de pintade aux truffes et poireaux*

# PAN-ROASTED GUINEA FOWL WITH TRUFFLES & LEEK

*Preparation time 40 minutes*
*Cooking time 15 minutes*

4 breasts of guinea fowl (or chicken if you prefer)

2 small black winter truffles, thinly sliced

3 tbsp olive oil

1 leek or 3 baby leeks, green parts only, thinly sliced

300g/11oz small new potatoes, cut into 5mm/¼-in thick rounds

100g/3½oz pancetta, thinly sliced

2 chervil or flat-leaf parsley sprigs, roughly chopped

75g/2½oz butter

sea salt and freshly ground black pepper

Preheat the oven to 180°C/350°F/gas 4.

Slit the skin of the guinea fowl breasts and place 3 thin slices of truffle underneath. Fold the skin back over the breast and season both sides of it with salt and pepper. Cut the remaining truffle slices into thin julienne strips and set aside for the vegetables. Heat 2 tablespoons of the oil in an ovenproof frying pan over a medium heat, add the guinea fowl, skin-side down, and cook for 2–3 minutes, until golden – make sure the pan is not too hot so that the skin does not shrink back too much. Turn the guinea fowl over and cook for a further minute, then place in the oven for 8 minutes. When ready, remove the breasts from the oven, put on a plate, set aside and keep warm.

While the guinea fowl is in the oven, heat two pans of salted water until boiling, drop the leeks in one and cook for 1 minute. Drain, refresh in ice-cold water and drain once more. Put the potatoes into the other pan of boiling water, cook for 6 minutes, then add the pancetta and cook for a further 2 minutes. Drain, refresh in ice-cold water and drain again. Heat a frying pan over a medium heat, add the remaining olive oil, potatoes and pancetta and cook for 1–2 minutes, until golden brown. Add the leek, a pinch of the reserved truffle and the chervil to the frying pan, then drain off any fat, add 2–3 tablespoons of water and stir to make a sauce. Add the butter and the remaining truffle and cook until the butter has melted.

Cut each breast in half lengthways. Place some of the leek and potato mixture in the middle of each serving plate, put the guinea fowl on top and pour the truffle butter sauce over.

All over France, hunters and cooks have for centuries prized wild rabbit for its lean meat and rich flavour. My grandparents kept rabbits on their farm, so I grew up eating farmed rabbit meat regularly. Although it was often overlooked in the last few decades, this meat is becoming popular again and farmed rabbit is now widely available. It tastes like chicken but with a more gamey flavour – and it's both delicious and nutritious. Even if you've never tried rabbit before, give it a go – I'm sure you will enjoy it!

## *Lapin en cocotte au citron et à l'ail*

# RABBIT CASSEROLE WITH LEMON & GARLIC

*Preparation time 20 minutes, plus
  5 minutes marinating and making
  the stock and spinach
Cooking time 1 hour 10 minutes*

juice and zest of 1 lemon

2kg/4lb 8oz farmed rabbit, cut into
  8 pieces

90ml/3fl oz/⅓ cup olive oil

15g/½oz butter

4 garlic cloves, unpeeled and
  crushed with the flat edge of
  a knife or your hand

500ml/17fl oz/2 cups Chicken
  Stock (see page 18)

2 thyme or basil sprigs

sea salt and freshly ground black
  pepper

1 recipe quantity Buttered Spinach
  with Lemon Zest (see page 162),
  to serve

Preheat the oven to 180°C/350°F/gas 4. Put the lemon zest and juice in a large bowl, add the rabbit pieces and 2 tablespoons of the olive oil and season with salt and pepper. Leave to marinate for 5 minutes.

Heat the butter and the remaining olive oil in a flameproof casserole dish over a medium heat and sauté the rabbit pieces until golden brown, about 8–10 minutes on each side. (You may have to do this in 2 batches depending on the size of your dish.) Add the garlic and the lemon marinade to the pan and stir to deglaze – there will be a bit of a splash and some smoke. Allow the liquid to reduce for about 5 minutes or until it is slightly syrupy and coats the back of a spoon. You will be able to tell when it's ready if when you run 2 fingers down the back of the spoon the 2 lines don't immediately join. Add the stock and thyme. Bring to the boil, then transfer the casserole to the preheated oven and bake for 30–35 minutes.

Remove the rabbit from the casserole dish onto an ovenproof serving dish and keep warm in the oven. Return the casserole dish to the hob and bring the cooking liquid to the boil, then reduce the heat to low and simmer, uncovered, for about 3–5 minutes until it has the consistency of a light syrup.

Pour the sauce over the rabbit and serve with buttered spinach.

This is a dish that used to be on the table very often during the hunting season, as Papa went shooting twice a week. He was a very good shot and loved it, so we always had game to eat and a full freezer for the rest of the year. Preparing this dish was very much Maman's domain and speciality, but I used to help a lot and really enjoyed preparing the vegetables for the roast to come. This is a simple dish, but to get it right it requires attention and you need young game for tenderness. This version is only rubbed quickly with oil and sea salt and is missing a classic red wine marinade, which, generally, I would reserve for older game – *grand veneur*.

## *Cuisse de chevreuil en cocotte*
# VENISON CASSEROLE

*Preparation time 40 minutes*
*Cooking time 1 hour 20 minutes*

2 tbsp sea salt

4 tbsp sunflower oil

1 venison haunch, about 1.8kg/4lb, tied up with string by your butcher

2 carrots, peeled and cut in half then cut in half lengthways

2 shallots, peeled and cut into small pieces lengthways

1 small head of garlic, unpeeled and cut in half horizontally

1 large thyme sprig

2 tbsp brandy

40g/1½oz butter

freshly ground black pepper

pre-cooked chestnuts, to serve

Rub the sea salt and 2 tablespoons of the oil all over the venison.

Heat the remaining oil in a large casserole dish or cast iron pot over a medium heat and fry the venison for 15–18 minutes, turning constantly, until golden brown all around. Season with pepper, then add the carrots and shallots and continue cooking with the lid on, but not quite closed, to reduce the condensation. Lower the heat slightly so it does not burn.

After 30 minutes, stir in the garlic and thyme, then add the brandy to deglaze and flambé. To do this, light a match and incline the plan slightly at an angle away from you so the flames will take hold. (Make sure there are no children around.) Alternatively, let the liquid reduce by half during the cooking process by removing the lid.

Continue cooking the venison for another 20 minutes, uncovered if reducing the liquid now, checking regularly to make sure it stays nice and moist. If the venison starts to dry, cover the dish partially to retain some of the moisture. Remove the meat from the casserole dish, transfer to a warmed serving dish, set aside and keep warm.

You should have some lovely juice at the bottom of the casserole dish and your vegetables should be golden and almost glazed. Add the butter to them and stir until combined, then season with salt and pepper. Keep warm while you carve the venison.

Pour the sauce, what we call 'jus' in a professional kitchen, over the venison and serve with the roasted vegetables and chestnuts.

*Filets de carrelet meunière aux amandes*

*Filets de bar aux citrons caramelisés*

*Sole au beurre citronné et persil*

*Bar en croûte de sel avec salade d'endives à l'orange*

*Moules marinières à la citronnelle et au piment*

*Gambas sautées au beurre d'ail et piment*

*Bouillabaisse*

## Les Poissons et Les Fruits de Mer
# FISH & SHELLFISH

If you were to wander the coastal cities of France, you would stumble upon brasseries with some spectacular seafood. At the entrance you would probably see display tables of freshly caught fish and shellfish laid out on ice, and inside you might find a tank with live lobsters and crabs, ready to be chosen and cooked *à la minute*. When seafood is this fresh you don't need to do much with it – simply grillng or roasting and a little herb butter, such as Dover Sole with Lemon & Parsley Butter, is all it needs. When eating at home with family or friends, we often enjoy delicious all-in-one pots of seafood such as a Bouillabaisse or Moules Marinières with Lemongrass & Chilli – there's nothing quite like it.

Unlike most freshwater fish, salmon have the ability to move freely between rivers and oceans because their bodies can adjust to changes in salt content. When it's time to lay their eggs and let the cycle begin again, and they always know when it is, salmon make the treacherous journey home, swimming upstream, navigating their way over rocks and through waterfalls, dodging predators, travelling hundreds of miles to return to the exact place they were born. When I teach trainees, I often talk about how important it is to treat your ingredients with respect. In the salmon's case, I think they've earned it!

*Steak de saumon poêlé avec mayonnaise au citron vert et coriandre*

# PAN-ROASTED SALMON STEAKS WITH LIME & CORIANDER MAYONNAISE

*Preparation time 15 minutes, plus making the potatoes*
*Cooking time 10 minutes*

4 skinless salmon steaks, about 150g/5½oz each

2 tbsp olive oil

15g/½oz butter

sea salt and freshly ground black pepper

1 recipe quantity Warm Crushed Potatoes with Coriander & Lime (see page 163), to serve

### LIME & CORIANDER MAYONNAISE

100g/3½oz/generous ⅓ cup mayonnaise

1 small handful of coriander, leaves only, chopped

zest of 1 lime, plus extra for sprinkling

juice of ½ lime

To make the lime and coriander mayonnaise, put the mayonnaise, coriander and lime zest and juice in a small bowl. Season with salt and pepper and mix to combine. This gives the mayonnaise a deliciously light zing and makes the dish really colourful.

For the pan-roasted salmon, season the salmon steaks with salt and pepper. Heat the olive oil and butter in a large frying pan over a medium heat. When the butter is starting to get frothy, add the salmon steaks and cook for 4–5 minutes on each side until light golden.

Put the salmon steaks on four plates, top with the mayonnaise and sprinkle with extra lime zest. Serve immediately with warm crushed potatoes.

CHEF'S TIP: *Instead of pan-roasting the salmon, you could poach it. To do this, place a saucepan of salted water over a medium-high heat and bring to the boil, then throw in a few stalks of coriander and a peeled garlic clove, crushed with the flat edge of a knife or your hand. Reduce the heat to low, add the salmon and poach for 5 minutes until it flakes off the fork and is still slightly pink in the middle. This is a delicious and very healthy alternative to pan-roasting.*

Summer is the best time of the year to enjoy Dover sole, but the similarly named but unrelated lemon sole is more widely available – you can find it during most of the year – which means you can enjoy this dish all year round, too. For me, sole is sublime: elegant, firm and deliciously delicate, yet full of flavour. Although it is very versatile, sole actually needs nothing more than grilling and topping with a light, hazelnut-coloured herb butter to create perfection – pure and simple! This dish is delicious served with new potatoes and buttered spinach.

*Sole au beurre citronné et persil*

# DOVER SOLE WITH LEMON & PARSLEY BUTTER

*Preparation time 10 minutes*
*Cooking time 12 minutes*

4 skinless Dover sole or lemon sole fillets, about 150g/5½oz each

1 tbsp plain flour

2 tbsp olive oil

125g/4½oz butter, softened

juice and zest of 1 lemon

1 handful of flat-leaf parsley, leaves only, chopped

sea salt and freshly ground black pepper

Preheat the oven to 200°C/400°F/gas 6 and heat a ridged griddle pan or heavy-based frying pan over a medium heat.

Pat the sole dry with kitchen towel, put it in a shallow dish and dust lightly with the flour. When the griddle pan is hot, place the sole fillets on it, one at a time, and cook for 1 minute. Rotate the fish 90 degrees and cook for another 1 minute to create a crisscross pattern.

Drizzle a heavy-based baking tray with the olive oil. Arrange the sole on the tray, cooked side up, then place one-quarter of the butter on each, season with salt and pepper and finish in the preheated oven for 3–4 minutes or until golden brown. Remove the fish from the pan, set aside and keep warm.

Add the lemon juice and zest and parsley to the pan and combine with the butter. Divide the fish onto four plates, spoon the parsley butter over the top and serve.

If you are travelling through France, this fish can be rather confusing – in the North it is called *Bar* and in the South *Loup de Mer*, meaning 'the wolf of the sea' – probably due to the sea bass' voracity and its habit of hunting in groups. It is widely available, as it is farmed, but can be a little pricey. However, one farmed fish can happily feed at least two people. This recipe harmonizes the sweet acidity of caramelized lemon with the grassiness of basil oil – I think it might be one of my favourites.

*Filets de bar aux citrons caramelisés*

# FILLETS OF SEA BASS WITH CARAMELIZED LEMONS

*Preparation time 25 minutes, plus making the potatoes*
*Cooking time 20 minutes*

2 lemons, thinly sliced

90ml/3fl oz/⅓ cup olive oil

1 small handful of basil

2 tsp icing sugar

4 sea bass fillets, about 150g/5½oz each, skins on

12 cherry tomatoes

basil infused olive oil, for drizzling

sea salt and freshly ground black pepper

1 recipe quantity Sautéed Potatoes with Parsley & Garlic (see page 163), to serve

Preheat the oven to 180°C/350°F/gas 4. Put the lemon slices on a baking tray, season with salt and pepper and drizzle 2 tablespoons of the olive oil over. Cover with the basil leaves and leave to marinate for 5 minutes.

Heat a ridged griddle pan, or heavy-based frying pan, over a medium heat. Dust the lemon slices on one side only with the icing sugar and place them on the pan, sugar side down. Cook for about 1–2 minutes until caramelized and golden, being careful not to burn the lemon – lower the heat, if necessary, as the sugar will colour quickly. Transfer to a baking dish and set aside.

Season the fish with salt and pepper, drizzle with 2 tablespoons of the remaining olive oil and put on the ridged griddle pan, skin-side down. Cook for 1 minute, then rotate 90 degrees and cook for a further 1 minute on the same side to create a crisscross pattern.

Put the fish on top of the lemon, then add the cherry tomatoes to the dish and season with salt and pepper. Drizzle with the remaining olive oil and cook the fillets in the preheated oven for 8 minutes until the skin is slighty crispy and the flesh is white and still moist when tested with the tines of a fork.

Serve the sea bass sprinkled with the basil oil and accompanied with sautéed potatoes with parsley and garlic.

This is a typical brasserie dish found all over France and can be made with either sea bass or sea bream. When baking in a sea salt crust, it is always better to cook the whole fish rather than fillets because it makes the flavour so much better. It is slightly less practical because you have to pick out the bones afterwards – but what you lose in convenience you gain in flavour. The combination of the fish with the chicory and citrus salad makes this a light, refreshing dish that zings! And don't worry about the salt content – it's just a casing to bring out the flavour.

*Bar en croûte de sel avec salade d'endives à l'orange*

# SEA BASS BAKED IN SEA SALT WITH CHICORY & ORANGE SALAD

*Preparation time 30 minutes*
*Cooking time 15 minutes*

2 egg whites

juice and zest of ½ lime

zest of ½ orange

1.8kg/4lb rock sea salt

1 whole sea bass, about 1.3kg/3lb, gutted

olive oil, for drizzling

sea salt and freshly ground black pepper

**CHICORY & ORANGE SALAD**

1 orange (ideally a blood orange, if available)

2 heads of yellow chicory

2 heads of purple chicory

½ small handful of dill, roughly chopped

2 tbsp olive oil

½ tbsp reduced balsamic vinegar

Preheat the oven to 190°C/375°F/gas 5. Put the egg whites in a large mixing bowl and whisk until stiff peaks form when the whisk is lifted from the bowl. Add a squeeze of lime juice, the lime and orange zests and the salt and mix by hand, or with a spatula if you prefer. Line a baking tray with greaseproof paper and spoon one-quarter of the salt mixture over it in a layer. Place the sea bass on the salt, then cover it completely with the remaining salt mix, pressing the salt down firmly around the fish.

Bake the fish in the preheated oven for 15 minutes, then remove and leave to rest for 2 minutes without touching the salt crust.

Meanwhile, prepare the salad. Grate the orange zest and set aside, then peel the orange and cut the segments from between the membrane. Do this over a bowl to catch the juices, adding the segments to the bowl.

Cut off the base and outer leaves of the chicory, then cut each head in half, lengthways, and remove the core. Put in a separate bowl. Add the orange zest, dill and oil and mix until combined. Just before serving, add the reduced balsamic vinegar, 2 tablespoons of the reserved orange juice and half the orange segments. (Adding the acidic ingredients at the last minute is essential to keep the salad fresh and crunchy.) Season with pepper and whisk until well combined.

To serve, break the top of the salt crust by knocking it gently with a wooden spoon. Remove the skin from the fish (it may come off with the crust). Lift the top fillet of fish off the bone with a fork and put it on a warm serving plate (one fillet should be enough for 2 people). Remove the bone from the fish, revealing the second fillet underneath, and transfer it to the serving plate. Drizzle with oil and season with salt and pepper. Serve immediately with the salad for a light, fresh and colourful dish.

I often cook sea bream for demos at food festivals and on TV because I think it is underrated and it isn't a fish that people necessarily think of eating at home. This is a great pity because it has lovely white flesh, a firm texture similar to that of sea bass and is perfect for steaming, grilling, baking and frying – in fact, for most types of Mediterranean cooking. Sea bream is available most of the year, so why not give it a try? You'll be pleasantly surprised.

*Filets de daurade, ragoût de pommes de terre et oignons avec sauce vierge*

# FILLETS OF SEA BREAM WITH POTATO & SPRING ONION RAGOÛT & SAUCE VIERGE

*Preparation time 15 minutes, plus making the sauce*
*Cooking time 30 minutes*

350g/12 oz small potatoes, such as Ratte, Charlotte, New or Jersey Royal

1 small fennel bulb

200g/7oz pancetta, cut into 5mm/¼in thin strips

4 sea bream fillets, 150g/5½oz each, pin-boned and skins on

1 tbsp olive oil

1 bunch of spring onions, peeled and finely sliced

sea salt and freshly ground black pepper

1 recipe quantity Sauce Vierge (see page 21), kept warm, to serve

Preheat the oven to 180°C/350°F/gas 4. Bring a large saucepan of salted water to the boil and cook the potatoes and fennel over a medium-low heat for 15 minutes. The potatoes should still be firm as you will sauté them later. Drain, peel the potatoes and cut into thick slices. Discard the fennel.

Bring another saucepan of water to the boil and blanch the pancetta for 30 seconds to remove the excess salt. Refresh in cold water, then drain and set aside on kitchen towel.

Season the sea bream fillets with salt and pepper. Heat a heavy-based frying pan over a medium heat and cook the fillets, skin-side down, for 4 minutes or until the skins start to turn crispy. Transfer the fish to an oven tray, skin side down, then place in the preheated oven and cook for a further 6 minutes until the flesh is white and still moist.

Meanwhile, make the ragoût. Heat the olive oil in the frying pan over a medium heat, then carefully add the prepared potatoes and pancetta. Cook for about 5 minutes until the potatoes are starting to turn golden, then add the spring onions and sauté for a further 2 minutes. Be careful not to break up the potatoes. Gently warm the sauce vierge while making the ragoût.

Divide the potato and spring onion ragoût onto four plates, arrange the fish on top, drizzle with the sauce and serve.

If you are using large red mullet, you will need to ask your fishmonger to scale and gut them, but with the smaller ones gutting is not necessary because they have nothing inside except the liver. If you were a French fisherman, you would probably just scale them in the sea water and cook them on board with a camping stove. If you are at home, it is not so different – simply pan-fry with garlic, thyme and a squeeze of lemon. Lovely!

*Rouget petit bateau poêlé au thym*

# PAN-FRIED RED MULLET WITH THYME

*Preparation time 20 minutes, plus
   making the potatoes
Cooking time 15 minutes*

4 garlic cloves, unpeeled

1 tbsp olive oil

4 whole red mullet, about 175g/6oz
   each, scaled and gutted by your
   fishmonger, or 8 fillets, skins on

25g/1oz butter

1 handful of thyme sprigs

juice of ½ lemon

sea salt and freshly ground black
   pepper

1 recipe quantity Warm Crushed
   Potatoes with Coriander & Lime
   (see page 163), to serve

Preheat the oven to 180°C/350°F/gas 4. Bring a saucepan of water to the boil and blanch the garlic for 3–4 minutes. This will ensure that it cooks in the same time as the fish. Drain and pat dry with kitchen towel.

If using whole fish, heat the olive oil in a large, heavy-based frying pan over a medium heat. Season the whole fish with salt and pepper, then add them and the garlic to the pan. Cook for 2 minutes or until the skin is a lovely golden colour. Turn the fish over, add the butter and thyme and cook for a further 2 minutes. Transfer to a baking tray and bake in the preheated oven for 3–4 minutes or until the flesh starts to break up. Remove from the oven, drizzle the fish with the lemon juice and season with salt and pepper.

If using fillets, heat the olive oil in large, heavy-based frying pan over a medium heat. Season the fish with salt and pepper, then add to the pan, skin side down, along with the garlic, thyme and butter. Cook for 2 minutes or until the skin is a lovely golden colour. Transfer to a baking tray and bake in the preheated oven for 2 minutes or until the flesh starts to break up. Remove from the oven, drizzle the fish with the lemon juice and season with salt and pepper.

Serve 1 whole fish or 2 fillets per person with warm crushed potatoes.

# Les Poissons et Les Fruits de Mer
# Fish & Shellfish

The topic of fish and shellfish is almost as vast as the sea itself, and one that I have a particular love for. It is my favourite subject and section in the kitchen. My brother Patrick and I used to go fishing in the river when we were young. We'd pack a *casse-croûte*, or snack, along with worms or bread for bait, and set off early in the morning, often to the same spot. We were fishing for *perche soleil*, a fish named for its rainbow-like colour. Sometimes we were lucky, sometimes not, but we always enjoyed the peace and quiet of a misty morning and the chance to chat. Patrick was always with me, good company and very funny. Most of the time we came back empty-handed or with just a few gudgeon, enough only for a small fried dish, but we were always happy to have spent some time together.

When learning my trade, I went to Brittany for a summer season. I was very young, maybe 16 or 17, and I recall the restaurant was in a small fishing village called Raguenes, right on the beach. When I think back, I know this is where my love for fish and seafood comes from. Sometimes I went with the owner of the restaurant to a very small island called 'Île Verte' to drop lobster traps. It was a prime spot for a great catch, and one that was passed on to him by his father. A few days later, we would go back and pull up the traps, then cook the lobster according to the family recipe, which was lovely. I have kept that recipe well under wraps ever since and only cook it that way at home. It is delicious.

Every morning, local fishermen would come to the door with a massive quantity of fish, the quality of which was unbelievable. One of the most popular was sea bass, a very meaty fish with firm flesh, which is equally delicious whether grilled, pan-fried, braised or baked. Versatile and tasty, they are available all year round, although it's best to avoid them in March to June when they are spawning. Other favourites were sardines – nutritious oily fish, which we grilled or barbecued whole, or made into *bouillabaisse*; and

ling, which are perfect in fish pie. These days they are much in demand and therefore overfished, so I only buy them if they are line-caught and have them occasionally as a treat.

The sustainability of fish is a big issue these days and one that we all need to consider. In my restaurant we try to make sure that we buy from a sustainable source. It is very important that we find the right suppliers who will provide us with the best possible fish that is also sourced from sustainable stocks. It is too easy to forget that most species are overfished, and therefore becoming not only expensive but increasingly rare. So, for example, we buy hand-dived scallops, not dredged ones, line-caught not net-caught fish, and farmed but organically reared fish, wherever possible.

Of course, I want my son's generation to be able to enjoy eating fish not only now but in the future. That is why it is important not only for us to protect our fish stocks, but also learn to respect the product. In my kitchen, we try to do just that by teaching our staff how to scale, gut and cut a fish properly and how to prepare seafood. Too often, you buy fish and shellfish that were badly damaged by not being handled properly. But I love going to the fishmonger and seeing the eye-catching display of fish that shows the rightful care it was given. The colourful line-up, the shine and the presence – it is beautiful and you know you will enjoy preparing, cooking and eating the fish you buy there.

I can't stress enough how necessary it is to buy fresh, quality produce from a good source. A fish should be firm to the touch and its skin and eyes should look bright – dullness or discolouration denote it is past its best. And smell it – a fresh fish has a 'clean', not overly 'fishy' odour, and sea fish often smell slightly salty or like seaweed. Lobsters and crabs should look undamaged and feel heavy for their size, while shellfish should have tightly closed shells.

In my restaurant I go round the tables to talk to my customers and often, when I discuss fish with them, they say they don't like it because they had bad experiences with it in the past. If this sounds like you, I encourage you to try again. I have challenged and, I hope, changed many people's negative attitudes toward fish and shellfish over the years. If you buy fresh fish or shellfish, prepare it in the right way and follow one of the recipes in this book, I bet you will experience great pleasure from eating it! Before you know it you will be eating fish regularly, which is great for your health – it's a great source of many nutrients, especially oily fish, which contain brain-boosting omega-3 fatty acids. At home we have fish as often as possible. I prefer it to meat anytime! Well… except perhaps for a Sunday roast.

I've included a lot of fish recipes in this book, all different and all, I hope, interesting. Some I have created myself over the years; others I've eaten or found elsewhere and they have inspired me to make my own version. The recipes are drawn from all over France and show you many ways of cooking fish and shellfish. From classic grilled Dover sole, baked sea bream and traditional bouillabaisse to mussels, scallops, clams, crabs, langoustines, plaice, salmon, monkfish, John Dory, tiger prawns, anchovies and many more, they are all here – a veritable feast from the sea!

You will probably already be familiar with some of the fish I include in my recipes – for example, the beautiful mackerel with its blue-black stripes, full of omega-3 fatty acids and packed with goodness. It is delicious grilled, smoked, pan-roasted, whole or in fillet form. You will also know tuna, which I really like. I adore blue-fin tuna, but as this fish is very rare I only buy it farmed; instead I have yellow-fin or skipjack. I love tuna raw, pan-fried or marinated and eat it often as it is available all year round. Other fish you probably will be acquainted with are haddock and hake, which are both very popular in France. Haddock belongs to the cod family but is smaller than cod. The flesh is white and delicate and it is usually sold as a whole fish or in fillets. Like cod, over the years it has been overfished, so to help protect the stocks, it's best to have it only occasionally. Hake has lovely white flesh and is very good in *gratin* dishes or pan-fried with butter sauces, such as Grenobloise.

I hope you will discover some new fish among the recipes in this book, too, such as pollack, which is now becoming a popular alternative to or substitute for cod and haddock. Found in the Atlantic Ocean along the coast of Brittany and as far south as the Bay of Biscay, this fish has a fine texture and can be cooked as steaks, deep fried, baked *en papillotte* or prepared as salt cod. It can be found all year round but is best avoided in January to April, when it is spawning. Black bream is increasingly widely available and can be found in any fish market. Its soft, white, dense flesh is succulent. I love it grilled whole or baked in sea salt. As always, line-caught is best, but it is also widely available farmed. And how about turbot? This flatfish lives on the sandy pebbly beds of the Atlantic Ocean. It has beautiful white, transparent flesh and is very firm to the touch. It is quite an expensive fish, so it is great for special occasions. Very versatile, it can be poached, roasted, steamed or pan-fried. Again, it is best to buy farmed or line-caught turbot whenever possible, or use its cousin brill, which is less under threat.

Lastly, I'd very much like you to try red mullet. Another fish that's very popular in France, red mullet is possibly my favourite fish of all. It's very delicate, has a strong 'sea rock' flavour, firm flesh and is a beautiful light pink colour. It can be baked, shallow-fried or cooked *en papillote*, but some of the best red mullet I've tasted has been simply grilled whole or in fillets. Delicious!

LEFT PAGE FROM TOP: red gunard
(rockfish), mackerel, tiger prawns, sea bass,
red mullet, pollack

RIGHT PAGE FROM TOP: plaice, John Dory,
sardines, black bream, langoustines

One of the best-known and loved flatfish of all, plaice can be easily identified at the fishmonger's by its distinctive brown colouring and vivid orange spots. If cooked well, this tasty fish can be every bit as good as Dover sole, and it is a much cheaper alternative, too. This recipe helps to bring out the natural meatiness of the fish and is one found on brasserie menus across France, perhaps not always with almonds, but certainly *à la meunière*. Who can resist it?

*Filets de carrelet meunière aux amandes*

# PAN-FRIED FILLETS OF PLAICE WITH BUTTER & ALMONDS

*Preparation time 15 minutes*
*Cooking time 15 minutes*

4 plaice fillets, about 125g/4½oz each

2 tbsp plain flour

55g/2oz butter

2 tbsp olive oil

20g/¾oz/¼ cup flaked almonds

1 handful of flat-leaf parsley, leaves only, finely chopped

juice of ½ lemon

sea salt and freshly ground black pepper

Put the fillets on a chopping board, season with salt and pepper and sprinkle with flour. Pat them briefly with kitchen towel to remove any excess flour, so there is just a fine dusting left on the fish.

Melt half the butter with the olive oil in a large, heavy-based frying pan over a medium-low heat. When the butter begins to foam, add the fillets and cook for 4–5 minutes on each side until they are a lovely golden colour and firm to the touch. Put the fillets on a plate, set aside and keep warm while you finish the butter sauce.

Add the remaining butter and the flaked almonds to the pan and cook until just golden. Throw in the parsley, pour the lemon juice over and season with salt and pepper.

Divide the fillets onto four plates, then pour the nutty, buttery sauce over and serve.

At home I do a lot of fish *en papillotte* because it is quick, easy and full of flavour – a good everyday option. 'En papillotte' simply means 'cooked in parcels', so all the flavour and goodness are locked inside. When you open up the parcel, you release a rush of aromas that take you on a journey without ever leaving your kitchen. You can make so many variations of this dish: ginger and lemongrass, chilli and coriander, lemon and basil, or lime and parsley. Experiment – you won't be disappointed.

*Filets de morue en papillotte à la coriandre, ail et tomate*

# COD, CORIANDER, TOMATO & GARLIC PARCELS

*Preparation time 20 minutes, plus making the rice*
*Cooking time 20 minutes*

4 pieces skinless, boneless cod fillet, about 150g/5½oz each

4 garlic cloves, unpeeled

4 tbsp olive oil

2 large tomatoes, sliced

1 small handful of coriander, leaves only, chopped

sea salt and freshly ground black pepper

steamed or boiled rice mixed with a handful of chopped coriander leaves, to serve

Preheat the oven to 200°C/400°F/gas 6 and bring a small saucepan of lightly salted water to the boil. Pat the fish dry with kitchen towel, season with salt and set aside.

Blanch the garlic in the boiling water for 2 minutes, then refresh in cold water and pat dry. That way it will cook in the same time as the fish once it is *en papillotte*.

Put four 46 x 25cm/18 x 10in rectangles of greaseproof paper on your work surface and drizzle them with half the olive oil. Next, you need to arrange the ingredients on one half of the paper, so that you will be able to fold the other half over them afterwards. Start with a few slices of tomato on each piece of paper and divide half the coriander over them, then season with salt and pepper. Put the pieces of cod fillet on top of the tomatoes, then add the blanched garlic and the rest of the coriander and drizzle with the remaining olive oil. Fold the paper over the filling and then fold along the edges to seal securely. Make sure the parcels are well sealed so that none of the liquid is lost. Put the parcels on a baking tray and bake for 15 minutes. Remove from the oven and leave to rest for 2 minutes before opening.

Now comes the rush of aromas – open each parcel, taking care not to lose any of the juices, and serve with coriander-scented rice. Squeeze the tender garlic out of its skin for an extra delicious flavour.

CHEF'S TIP: *If sustainable cod is not available, replace with pollack fillets.*

When a dish has olives in it, more often than not it comes from the South of France. I love olives, so it follows that I love the food from the south, and I couldn't resist including this recipe. It's a great classic from Nice and a firm favourite everywhere. As an alternative, for something a little different, it can also be made with artichokes and broad beans. Either way, it's full of exhilarating fresh flavours and vibrant colour.

## *Salade niçoise*
# NIÇOISE SALAD

*Preparation time 30 minutes*
*Cooking time 55 minutes*

1 red pepper

320g/11¼oz small potatoes such as Ratte, Charlotte, New or Jersey Royal

200g/7oz green beans, trimmed

4 eggs or 8 quail eggs

4 tomatoes, cut into wedges

1 white or red onion, sliced into fine rings

80g/2¾oz/scant ⅔ cup black pitted olives, or green if preferred

100g/3½oz anchovies in oil, drained

250g/9oz fresh tuna steaks (from a sustainable source)

sea salt and freshly ground black pepper

**DRESSING**

1 large shallot, finely chopped

2 garlic cloves, finely sliced

90ml/3fl oz/⅓ cup olive oil, plus extra for frying

2 tbsp red wine vinegar

Preheat the oven to 200°C/400°F/gas 6, then cook the whole pepper for 30 minutes. Remove from the oven and place in a bowl. Cover with cling film and leave to cool.

Bring three saucepans of salted water to the boil. In one pan, cook the potatoes for 15–20 minutes until tender and you can easily push a sharp knife through them. Drain and set aside until cool enough to handle.

Meanwhile, cook the green beans for 10 minutes in the second pan, then refresh under cold running water so they keep their form and colour. In the third pan, hardboil the eggs for 8 minutes or quail eggs for 4 minutes, then drain and leave to cool.

To make the dressing, whisk the shallot, garlic, oil and vinegar together in a small bowl. Season with salt and pepper and set aside.

Peel, deseed and slice the pepper lengthways. Peel the potatoes and cut them into thick slices and peel the eggs and cut into quarters (if using quail eggs, cut them in half only). Arrange the peppers, tomatoes, onion and the eggs on a large, deep plate and top with the olives and anchovies.

Season the tuna with salt and pepper. Heat a large frying pan over a medium heat. Add a little olive oil, then add the tuna and cook for 1–2 minutes on each side until browned on the outside but still rare in the middle. Put the tuna on top of the salad, pour the dressing over and serve immediately.

Saffron is one of the most expensive and treasured spices in the world. It takes around 4,300 crocus flowers to produce just 28g (1oz) of saffron, and the thread-like stigmas are hand-picked. Fortunately, its intensity, flavour and colour mean that the smallest amount brings an incredible aroma and flavour to this dish.

*Pavé de lotte rôtie, ragoût de moules et palourdes au safran*

# ROAST MONKFISH FILLET WITH SAFFRON-SCENTED MUSSEL & CLAM RAGOÛT

*Preparation time 35 minutes, plus cooking the rice and asparagus*
*Cooking time 30 minutes*

1 monkfish fillet, about 400g/14oz, skinless and boneless

400g/14oz fresh mussels

200g/7oz fresh clams or cockles

2 tbsp olive oil

55g/2oz butter

1 shallot, finely chopped

a pinch of saffron threads

100ml/3½fl oz/scant ½ cup double cream, half of it whipped

zest of 1 lime

1 small handful of chives, roughly chopped

sea salt and freshly ground black pepper

steamed rice, to serve

cooked asparagus, to serve

Preheat the oven to 200°C/400°F/gas 6. Wrap the monkfish in a clean tea towel and set aside. This will absorb excess liquid and make it easier to roast.

Remove and discard the beards from the mussels and wash them and the clams in a bowl under running cold water, scrubbing well to remove all traces of grit. Discard any that float or any open ones that do not close when tapped. Set aside.

Put half the oil and butter in an ovenproof frying pan over a medium heat. When the butter begins to foam, add the monkfish and cook for 4–5 minutes, turning continuously, until it has a lovely golden colour all over. Transfer to the preheated oven and roast for 8 minutes until firm to the touch. Remove from the oven, transfer to a clean dish, cover with kitchen foil and set aside.

Put the remaining oil and butter in a cast iron or heavy-based pan over a medium heat. When the butter is foaming, add the shallot and cook for 1 minute, stirring, then add the mussels, cockles and saffron. Cover and cook for 4–5 minutes or until the shellfish open. Discard any mussels or cockles that remain closed.

Pour the unwhipped cream into the pan with the shellfish and cook, uncovered, over a medium to high heat, for 2 minutes. Remove from the heat, use a slotted spoon to take the shellfish out of the pan and put them in a large bowl, then cover and set aside. Return the pan with the cooking liquid to a medium heat and cook for 4–5 minutes until reduced by half. Stir in the whipped cream and cook for a further 2–3 minutes. Remove from the heat, add the lime zest, chives and any juices that have collected from the monkfish and season with salt and pepper. You should now have about 100ml/3½fl oz/scant ½ cup sauce.

Slice the monkfish into 4 pieces and either divide onto four plates with the ragoût and a few spoonfuls of the sauce spooned over it or place in a casserole dish to serve at the table with steamed rice and asparagus.

Bouillabaisse, an elaborate fish soup from Marseilles in the South of France, is the very essence of the sea. Originally the food of poor fishermen, who put in it whatever they hadn't been able to sell that day, it has evolved into a voluptuous mix of succulent fish and shellfish, made enticing with herbs, spices and vegetables.

## *Bouillabaisse*
# BOUILLABAISSE

*Preparation time 20 minutes*
*Cooking time 55 minutes*

4 tbsp olive oil

1 large onion, chopped

1 leek, finely sliced and rinsed

1 fennel bulb, chopped

3 tomatoes, peeled and chopped

2 tbsp tomato purée

4 garlic cloves, peeled and crushed with the flat edge of a knife or your hand

1 thyme sprig

a large pinch of saffron threads

1.8kg/4lb fish and shellfish such as follows:
  4 large langoustines or tiger prawns, crushed with a rolling pin
  2 rascasse, grey mullet or black bream, scaled, gutted and cut into portions
  2 John Dory or lemon sole, scaled, gutted and cut into portions
  4 slices of hake, pollack, haddock or ling
  4 small red mullet or red bream, scaled and gutted

4 tbsp white wine

2 tbsp aniseed-flavoured spirit, such as Pastis or Pernod

1 handful of flat-leaf parsley, leaves only, roughly chopped

sea salt and freshly ground black pepper

crusty farmhouse bread, to serve

Heat a little of the oil in a large, heavy-based or cast iron casserole pan over a medium heat and cook the onion, leek and fennel for 4–5 minutes, stirring occasionally. Add the tomatoes, tomato purée, garlic, thyme and saffron and cook for a further 2 minutes, stirring occasionally. Add the langoustines and stir until they are a deep orange colour. Add the wine and spirit and stir to deglaze. Add 1l/35fl oz/4 cups water and cook for a good 30 minutes, by which time the soup will already have a great flavour and rich colour. Strain and press the mixture through a colander into a clean saucepan that is large enough to hold all the fish you are about to add. Discard anything that remains of the langoustines.

Return the soup to a medium heat, add all the fish, except the red mullet, and cook for 7–8 minutes. Add the red mullet and cook for a further 6 minutes, then season with salt and pepper. Remove from the heat, stir in the parsley and serve hot with crusty farmhouse bread.

CHEF'S TIPS: *Ask your fishmonger to prepare all the fish for you – don't be shy, that is what he or she is there for. Get him or her to scale, debone and gut whatever you like, and to cut the big fish into portions – except for the red mullet and the langoustines, which should be kept whole.*

*If you want to make it a hearty and more complete meal, add 500g/1lb 2oz peeled potatoes, cut into large cubes, to the fish bouillon when you add the first batch of fish – they will soak up all the goodness too.*

Scallops are sublime – I don't think I know anyone who doesn't like them. If you live near a harbour and can get hold of hand-dived, day-boat scallops, then snap them up! When scallops are dredged, they are usually full of sand or mud, which has an enormous effect on their flavour, but if they are hand-dived you won't have that problem. You can do this recipe by simply roasting the scallops, but they are much tastier cooked in the shell – and it is a fun way to serve it, too.

*Noix de Saint-Jacques au beurre de curry et herbes*

# SCALLOPS WITH CURRY & HERB BUTTER

*Preparation time 15 minutes*
*Cooking time 6 minutes*

16 large scallops in their shells, trimmed by your fishmonger

1 tsp mild curry powder

2 small garlic cloves, finely chopped

1½ handfuls of chervil, finely chopped

1½ handfuls of chives, finely chopped

150g/5½oz butter, softened

juice of 1 lemon

sea salt and freshly ground black pepper

cooked asparagus, to serve (optional)

baguette, to serve (optional)

Preheat the grill to medium.

Season the scallops with salt and pepper and a light dusting of curry powder, then put them on a baking tray.

Put the garlic, chervil, chives and butter in a bowl and mix together. Divide the mixture between the scallops, then place under the grill and cook for 5–6 minutes or until the butter is golden brown. Squeeze a few drops of lemon juice over each scallop.

Serve immediately. Delicious with asparagus and fresh baguette.

Whether grilled, sautéed, pan-roasted or cooked in a bouillon, tiger prawns are quick, easy and delicious. In brasseries in France, they are taken fresh from the tank and sautéed with sea salt. When cooking at home, you will need to buy them shelled from your fishmonger (make sure they're deveined). Try to avoid frozen prawns if you can – as always with seafood, it is not worth compromising on the freshness.

*Gambas sautées au beurre d'ail et piment*

# SAUTÉED TIGER PRAWNS WITH CHILLI & GARLIC BUTTER

*Preparation time 10 minutes*
*Cooking time 6 minutes*

8 large or 24 small raw tiger prawns, shelled and deveined

2 tbsp olive oil

85g/3oz butter

1 red chilli, deseeded and finely chopped

2 garlic cloves, unpeeled and crushed with the flat edge of a knife or your hand and finely chopped

1 small handful of flat-leaf parsley, leaves only, finely chopped

juice and zest of 1 lime

salt and freshly ground black pepper

Wash the prawns and dry them on kitchen towel. Warm the oil and 30g/1oz of the butter in a heavy-based frying pan over a medium heat. When the butter is foaming, throw in the prawns and sauté for 4 minutes. Remove from the pan and set aside.

Add the remaining butter, chilli, garlic and parsley to the frying pan. When the butter is foaming, put the prawns back in the pan and toss for 1–2 minutes. Season with salt and pepper to taste, add a few drops of lime juice and sprinkle with the freshly grated lime zest, then serve immediately. Simple and delicious.

One of the great classics of French cuisine – my version is with a hint of the East, something I developed a taste for while working in Singapore. One very important thing with mussels is quality and freshness. A good way to see if you have any bad ones is to wash them in a bowl under running cold water, and if any float to the surface, get rid of them. It is a sign that they are not fresh. As for the rest, remove the beards and wash them until there is no grit on the bottom of the bowl.

*Moules marinières à la citronnelle et au piment*

# MOULES MARINIÈRES WITH LEMONGRASS & CHILLI

*Preparation time 15 minutes*
*Cooking time 6 minutes*

2kg/4lb 8oz fresh mussels

1 tbsp olive oil

30g/1oz butter

1 shallot, finely chopped

30g/1oz ginger, peeled and thinly sliced

1 red chilli, deseeded and cut into thick slices

2 lemongrass stalks, halved and bruised

4 tbsp coconut milk

4 tbsp whipped cream

1 handful of coriander, leaves only, chopped

sea salt and freshly ground black pepper

Remove and discard the beards from the mussels and wash them in a bowl under cold running water, scrubbing to remove all traces of grit. Discard any that float or any open ones that don't close when tapped.

Heat the oil and butter in a large saucepan over a low heat. When the butter begins to foam, add the shallot, ginger, chilli and lemongrass and cook for 2 minutes. Add the mussels and coconut milk and cover with a lid. Cook for 4 minutes or until the mussels open. Discard any that remain closed.

Remove from the heat and add the whipped cream and coriander and season with salt and pepper. Serve immediately, in a large bowl placed in the middle of the table for everyone to share.

*Risotto au citron vert*

*Quiche au Roquefort, brocolis et oignon*

*Tian de légumes à la Provençale*

*Tarte à la tomate et au fromage de chèvre*

*Omelette aux girolles et aux herbes*

*Ratatouille à la Provençale*

*Tarte aux artichauts, oignons et thym*

## Les Plats Végétariens
# VEGETARIAN DISHES

The fresh produce in French markets in summer is inspiring. The abundance of fruit and vegetables the warm weather brings makes creating vegetarian recipes easy. You can spread tomatoes in a light pastry case and cover them with goat's cheese for a crunchy tomato tart, or layer vegetables in a baking dish with garlic and herbs and create a Provençal Vegetable Gratin. There are risottos, crêpes, vegetable tagines and, of course, the world famous ratatouille. France often gets a bad press when it comes to vegetarian food, but this is changing and it is now often found on menus in brasseries.

This colourful Mediterranean dish is ideal for those outdoor summer lunches. Make sure you choose a goat's cheese you love. One I really enjoy is Sainte-Maure de Touraine, a chèvre from the Loire region – it is well-balanced, smooth, slightly salty and has a lovely, nutty aroma. Tomatoes are a personal thing, too – choose the variety that really zings for you. For the topping you can use your own home-made, oven-dried tomatoes, or, if you are short on time, sun-dried tomatoes from a jar.

*Tarte à la tomate et au fromage de chèvre*

# TOMATO TART WITH GOAT'S CHEESE

*Preparation time 20 minutes, plus making the tomatoes and chilling Cooking time 50 minutes*

butter, for greasing

250g/9oz ready-made puff pastry

plain flour, for dusting

1 tbsp balsamic vinegar, plus extra to serve

12 Oven-dried Tomatoes (see page 41) or 12 sun-dried tomatoes from a jar, drained

85g/3oz goat's cheese, sliced

100g/3½oz rocket leaves, to serve

sea salt and freshly ground black pepper

2 tbsp olive oil, to serve

### TOMATO BASE

4 tbsp olive oil

½ onion, chopped

2 garlic cloves, finely chopped

1 large tomato, chopped

1 thyme sprig

1 tbsp reduced balsamic vinegar

To make the tomato base, heat 3 tablespoons of the olive oil in a medium saucepan over a medium heat. Add the onion and garlic and cook, partially covered, for 4–5 minutes, stirring occasionally, until softened. Add the tomato, thyme and the remaining olive oil, then reduce the heat to low and simmer for 35–40 minutes, stirring often to avoid browning or burning the tomato. If the mixture gets too dry, add a few tablespoons of water. Stir in the reduced balsamic vinegar and season with salt and pepper.

Meanwhile, preheat the oven to 180°C/350°F/gas 4 and grease a 20cm/8in tart tin with butter. Roll out the pastry on a lightly floured surface until it is about 3mm/⅛in thick and 25cm/10in in diameter. Line the tin with the pastry, taking care not to stretch it. Press down gently to push out any bubbles and roll the rolling pin along the top edge of the tin to trim off the excess pastry. Prick the base with a fork and chill for 25–30 minutes. This will prevent the pastry from shrinking during cooking.

Place the tart tin on a baking tray and bake in the preheated oven for 15 minutes or until golden. Remove from the oven and do not turn the oven off. Brush the pastry with the balsamic vinegar and then return it to the oven for a further 3 minutes. The vinegar will seal the top of the pastry and ensure that your tart is crunchy. Be careful not to overcook it or it will become dry and bitter.

To assemble the tart, remove the thyme sprig from the tomato base and spread the base over the pastry. Arrange the Oven-dried Tomatoes and goat's cheese on top and season with salt and pepper. Place the tart in the oven and bake for 3–4 minutes until the cheese starts to melt, but don't allow it to melt completely. If you want, you can flash it for 2 minutes under a grill, preheated to high, to give it a lovely colour.

Serve sprinkled with rocket and drizzled with oil and balsamic vinegar. *Voilà* – a gorgeous, light and colourful lunch.

Rich, spicy, blue-veined Roquefort is thought to be one of the greatest blue cheeses in the world, and the people of Roquefort protect it fiercely. They have been making it for thousands of years, since the time of ancient Rome, in fact. It proved so popular that imitations of it started to spring up all over the place until, in the 1960s, the *Tribunal de Grande Instance* decreed that, although similar cheeses could be made in many regions of France, it was only a true Roquefort if it had been ripened in the natural caves of Mont Combalou in Roquefort-sur-Soulzon.

*Quiche au Roquefort, brocolis et oignon*

# ROQUEFORT, BROCCOLI & ONION QUICHE

*Preparation time 20 minutes, plus making the pastry and chilling*
*Cooking time 1 hour 10 minutes*

15g/½oz butter, plus extra for greasing

plain flour, for dusting

250g/9oz Savoury Short Pastry (see page 23) or ready-made shortcrust pastry

2 tbsp olive oil

1 onion, finely chopped

175g/6oz broccoli, cut into small florets

2 eggs

210ml/7½fl oz/1 cup double cream

¼ tsp freshly grated nutmeg

100g/3½oz Roquefort cheese or other blue cheese of choice, crumbled

sea salt and freshly ground black pepper

salad, to serve

Grease a 20cm/8in tart tin with butter. Roll out the pastry on a lightly floured surface until it is about 3mm/⅛in thick and 25cm/10in in diameter. Line the tin with the pastry, taking care not to stretch it. Press down gently to push out any bubbles and roll the rolling pin along the edge of the tin to trim off the excess pastry. Prick the base with a fork and chill for 25–30 minutes.This will prevent the pastry from shrinking during cooking.

Meanwhile, make the filling. Heat the butter and oil in a medium frying pan over a medium heat and cook the onion for 10 minutes, stirring occasionally and making sure they don't brown. Set aside.

Bring a saucepan of salted water to the boil and blanch the broccoli for 5 minutes until al dente, then refresh in ice-cold water. Drain, pat dry with a clean tea towel and set aside.

Put the eggs, cream and nutmeg in a bowl and season with salt and pepper, then whisk to combine and set aside.

Preheat the oven to 170°C/325°F/gas 3. When the oven is hot, line the pastry case with baking parchment and fill with baking beans. Bake in the preheated oven for 12 minutes, then remove from the oven, discard the beans and parchment and turn the oven up to 180°C/350°F/gas 4.

To assemble the quiche, spread the onions over the pastry case. Sprinkle the Roquefort on top of the onion, then the broccoli. Pour in the egg mixture and bake for 35 minutes. To check for doneness, do the knife test – it should come out dry and warm. If it isn't ready, return the quiche to the oven for another 5 minutes and test again. Remove from the oven and set aside to cool.

Remove the quiche from the tin and serve with the salad of your choice. Delicious warm or cold.

Chanterelle mushrooms are really special. They have a lovely mild flavour and can be picked between late autumn and winter. They generally grow under hardwood and softwood trees, especially in older, moss-rich forests. A word of caution – if you decide to go foraging for them, take someone with you who knows what they are doing, or you might end up feeling a bit more special than you hoped, or very ill. If you are in any doubt at all, please don't eat them – you can buy beautiful chanterelles from most delicatessens.

*Omelette aux girolles et aux herbes*

# CHANTERELLE MUSHROOM & HERB OMELETTE

*Preparation time 15 minutes, plus 30 minutes marinating and making the salad*
*Cooking time 10 minutes*

200g/7oz chanterelle or brown mushrooms, trimmed

2 tbsp olive oil

a few drops of lemon juice

15g/½oz butter

1 handful of flat-leaf parsley, chopped

1 garlic clove, chopped

8 eggs, beaten

sea salt and freshly ground black pepper

green salad, to serve (optional)

Wash the mushrooms very carefully as they are fragile and break easily. Pat dry with kitchen towel. If the chanterelles are large, just cut them in half, but ideally use small, whole ones. Mix the oil and lemon juice together in a bowl, add the mushrooms and leave to marinate for 30 minutes.

Warm the butter in a large, non-stick frying pan over a medium heat. Drain the mushrooms and sauté them for 3–4 minutes or until they are a nice golden brown, then throw in the parsley and garlic and season with salt and pepper.

Add the eggs to the pan and cook the omelette for 3–4 minutes until it still has a slightly runny consistency in the centre. Tilt the pan slightly, and, with the help of a wooden spoon, carefully fold the edge of the omelette over, then roll it up. If you prefer your omelette well done, flip it over using a wooden spatula and cook for a further 3–4 minutes until pale golden.

Serve the omelette with a green salad, if liked, for a lovely, simple meal.

In France, chanterelles are never on the ground for long – people soon snap them up. But in Britain, people are more nervous about mushrooms being poisonous, so they often perish uneaten. I remember walking through the estate of Castle Kennedy in Scotland with my father, the path was lined with ancient trees and their moisture gave the ground that springy, mossy feeling. Suddenly my father stopped and rushed over to the other side of the path, guarding something fiercely with his body while smiling politely at passers-by, who walked on nervously. He then got down on his knees, took out his penknife and called me over. There on the ground were dozens of chanterelles, their yellow caps a little battered but nonetheless good enough to eat. We cut them, took them home and made an incredible omelette. This dish, along with my Chanterelle Mushroom & Herb Omelette (page 135) and Wild Mushroom & Herb Risotto (page 142), are all close to my heart.

*Crêpes aux champignons et estragon*

# CRÊPES WITH MUSHROOMS & TARRAGON

*Preparation time 15 minutes, plus making the crêpes and salad*
*Cooking time 10 minutes*

1 tbsp olive oil

250g/9oz button or wild mushrooms, sliced

15g/½oz butter

1 handful of tarragon, chopped

1 recipe quantity Basic Crêpes, made without sugar (see page 25)

sea salt and freshly ground black pepper

tomato, onion and flat-leaf parsley salad, or rocket salad, to serve

Preheat the oven to 180°C/350°F/gas 4. Warm the oil in a non-stick frying pan over a medium heat and sauté the mushrooms for 3–4 minutes or until the juices they release have reduced to a syrup. Add the butter and continue to cook for 2–3 minutes or until they are a lovely golden colour. Throw in the tarragon and season with salt and pepper.

Lay the crêpes on a baking tray, divide the mushroom mixture over them and roll them up like a wrap. Bake for 2–3 minutes just to warm through. Serve warm with salad.

# *Les Champignons Sauvages*
# *Wild Mushrooms*

As I write this, we are well into autumn, my favourite season. Where I lived in Franche-Comté, there are plenty of forests and I used to go there almost on a daily basis when I was growing up – I particularly loved the autumn when the trees changed colour. My father hunted and often took me with him, although not necessarily to shoot. In fact, we would chat or go on a long walk with our dogs while he told me about the deer. He knew all their habits and could spot them from a few hundred yards – well before I could. He was such a good observer of nature. He had a lot of patience, sometimes waiting for hours at a time just to see the deer. I wasn't surprised when, in his early fifties, my father stopped hunting, but he still took the dogs into the forest for hours. Now, however, he collected mushrooms – and our forest was full of them.

Mushroom pickers are secretive, and we only tell our family or trusted friends where to find the best sources. We worry about people going to the prime location behind our backs, and possibly giving it away to others, which could damage the area. Despite such efforts to keep mushroom locations secret, many people now go foraging. As a result, in France there are now restrictions on how many mushrooms you can pick and, in some areas, guards patrol to check that people are respecting the forest.

Quite often, I used to go foraging on my own with my dogs. One day just by getting lost on the wrong path, I found I had stepped on a few *trompettes de la mort*, or horn of plenty mushrooms. Suddenly, I looked around and there was a big patch of them in front of me. Generally picked from summer to autumn, *trompettes de la mort* are common woodland mushrooms resembling black funnels. They are slightly tough in texture and often chopped and added to a sauce or mixed with other mushrooms. They can also be dried. I like these mushrooms for their very earthy flavour.

Not far away from the Trompettes de la Mort, I also discovered a patch of *girolle* mushrooms (known, too, as chanterelles). Funnel-shaped, *girolles* are found mainly in hardwood and coniferous forests, especially in older, moss-rich forests, and are usually picked between June and October. They are an orange-yellow colour with a delicate stalk. With their nutty flavour, they are beautiful when pan-fried with herbs and served with pasta. Needless to say, I made sure I marked the spots where these mushroms grew and I returned there often to pick them.

There is nothing more satisfying than collecting mushrooms, bringing them home and cooking them. I particularly like *cèpes* (called *porcini* in Italian) with their large, bulbous stalks. They are best eaten young, and are delicious cooked in omelettes or velouté sauces. In France, the small ones of the highest quality are known as *bouchons*. There are plenty of *cèpes* in Britain – for example, in the New Forest – but they can also be found dried or in jars in oil.

There are also plenty of Scottish *girolles*, which are 2.5cm/1in tall, a bright yellow-orange colour and smell like apricots. When we went foraging, Papa and I were on our knees, picking very carefully so that the following year's crop would not be compromised. Papa always carried his knife (a hunter's habit, I suppose) folded in his back pocket, along with a plastic bag. I remember holding the *girolles* with bits of moss and leaves still clinging to them, bringing them to my nose and slowly breathing in their incredible scent of earth, apricots, dry leaf, forest and moist soil. Off we went home to prepare them and make the most gorgeous omelette ever. Those are precious memories – it was a brilliant time!

There are hundreds of common mushroom varieties apart from those I've already mentioned, such as button and brown mushrooms, but some of the tastiest include field mushrooms, *morilles* (morels), oyster mushrooms and blewits. Field mushrooms are found in summer and autumn in rich, open, manured grasslands grazed by horses or cows, and are white to pinkish grey with a white stem. These were my Maman's favourite and we used to get up at dawn to collect them. They are delicious sautéed with butter and herbs. Found in springtime, morels are very tasty. Their conical shape has a delightful honeycomb pattern and they have a delicate scent. I like them best cooked with a touch of cream and chopped chives. You can find dried morels in supermarkets and delicatessens. Oyster mushrooms prefer cold weather and are therefore found in late autumn and winter. They have a very mild flavour and are delicious fricasséed or sautéed with garlic or finished with cream on a steak. And blewits, which are a beautiful lilac colour, are found in late autumn in pine forests and near hedgerows. They go very well with strongly flavoured vegetables, such as onions.

When you go foraging you need to get up as early as possible and just get out and get looking! It is such a satisfying moment when you find a patch of wild mushrooms. And who knows, perhaps you will see a deer or two or other wild creatures on the way, or simply enjoy the colours of the forest and the crunching of the leaves under your feet. However, collecting and eating the wrong mushrooms can make you very sick, or even kill you, so before you start, you must learn about them. At first, go foraging with someone who knows what is edible and what is not. Once you have some experience, you can go on your own, but you should still take a good field guide with you, and always double-check that you've picked an edible variety. The golden rule is: *if you're not sure, don't eat it.* Prepare wild mushrooms carefully and wash them well. Slugs, snails and other unwanted inhabitants love them, too!

We have local foragers who supply us at The Vineyard, so it's almost as if we had our own patch. Mushrooms feature in my menu in the late summer, autumn and winter on a regular basis, and they're very popular. I prepare them in many different ways, such as in risottos, fricassées and purées; sautéed with herbs in omelettes and folded into soufflés. And of course, they feature in our all-truffle menu, which even includes an ice cream made with the most expensive and highly esteemed of all mushrooms – the black Périgord truffle. This delicacy matures after the first frost and is at its best after Christmas. Truffles are subterranean fungi, which live in symbiosis with certain trees, mainly the oak, but also the chestnut, hazel and beech tree. You can now buy them in tins or jars, peeled or scrubbed, ripe, whole or chopped. You can also freeze them. There are several ways of cooking them and they can also be eaten raw if finely sliced.

I don't think I know a chef who doesn't like mushrooms or cooking with them. They are so versatile and go well with many other ingredients, such as fish, shellfish, poultry and meat. Wild game with wild mushrooms is an especially good match – they are made for each other. Mushrooms are also a great option for vegetarians.

Wild mushrooms are readily available during their seasons, and if you don't pick them yourself you can find them in good supermarkets. They are usually also available dried in delicatessens and supermarkets all year round. The flavour, texture and scent of wild mushrooms are very distinct; cultivated mushrooms are more widely available but are no match for the unique appeal of their wild cousins!

LEFT PAGE FROM TOP: oyster mushrooms, shiitake mushrooms, pieds bleus (blewits), horn of plenty, girolles, yellow chanterelles

RIGHT PAGE FROM TOP: cèpes, morilles (morels), brown button mushrooms, button mushrooms

For this dish, I prefer the bouchon mushroom. These are small wild mushrooms, so called because they look like the cork of a champagne bottle. You can buy them dried from a deli, but porcini mushrooms will also do fine if you can't find bouchons. The mistake people often make with a risotto is to think you can leave it – you can't, not even for a minute – and this recipe is no different!

*Risotto aux champignons des bois*

# WILD MUSHROOM RISOTTO

*Preparation time 15 minutes, plus 45 minutes soaking and making the stock*
*Cooking time 35 minutes*

150g/5½oz fresh bouchon, shiitake or porcini mushrooms, or 20g/¾ oz dried porcini mushrooms

90g/3¼in oz butter

1 large shallot or small onion, very finely chopped

90ml/3fl oz/⅓ cup dry white wine

1l/35fl oz/4 cups Vegetable Stock (see page 19)

300g/10½oz/heaped 1⅓ cup risotto rice, such as arborio or carnaroli

1 tbsp crème fraîche

1½ tbsp chopped chives

sea salt and freshly ground black pepper

Parmesan cheese, to serve

If using fresh mushrooms, wash them very carefully as they are fragile and break easily. Then trim the foot and cut them lengthways. If using dried mushrooms, soak them in warm water for 45 minutes, then rinse and pat dry with kitchen towel.

Heat half the butter in a frying pan over a medium heat, add half the shallot and the mushrooms and sauté for 2 minutes until golden. Add a few tablespoons of the wine – it will make a great splashing sound – and let it evaporate a little. Season with salt and pepper and set aside.

Now make the risotto. Bring the stock to the boil, then reduce the heat to low and keep it at a simmer.

Melt the remaining butter in a large, heavy-based saucepan over a low heat and add the remaining shallot. Cook for 2–3 minutes or until softened but not browned, then add the rice and stir. Add the remaining wine and let it evaporate to remove the acidity. Add one ladleful of the stock and stir continuously until it is absorbed. Repeat until the rice is cooked, about 16–18 minutes. The grains should be plump but still firm and not too wet (having said that, risotto is a personal thing – I like mine quite loose and light). At the last minute, add the crème fraîche and finish by folding in the mushrooms and chives and seasoning with salt and pepper.

Serve immediately. Have a hunk of Parmesan cheese and a grater ready at the table in case your guests want to sprinkle some on top. Light and luscious!

If you think of artichokes, it is probably the green ones that spring to mind, but I also like to cook with purple artichokes, which are more often found in Provence. Because they are harder to find, they are so often overlooked, which is a pity. They are smaller and sweeter and, coupled with red peppers, bring vibrant colour to your dish. Finish the gratin with goat's cheese for a scrumptious seasonal delight.

*Gratin d'artichauts et poivrons rouges au fromage de chèvre*

# ARTICHOKE & RED PEPPER GRATIN WITH GOAT'S CHEESE

*Preparation time 20 minutes*
*Cooking time 1 hour 30 minutes*

juice of 1 lemon

2 large red peppers

18 small purple artichokes or 310g/11oz drained preserved artichoke hearts

4 tbsp olive oil

2 thyme sprigs

2 garlic cloves, unpeeled and crushed with the flat edge of a knife or your hand

4 tbsp dry white wine

sea salt and freshly ground black pepper

1 tsp chopped rosemary, leaves only, to serve

**GOAT'S CHEESE SAUCE**

400ml/14fl oz/scant 1⅔ cups double cream

125g/4½oz mild goat's cheese, crumbled

Preheat the oven to 200°C/400°F/gas 6 . Fill a large bowl with water and mix in the lemon juice.

Put the whole peppers on a baking sheet and roast for 40 minutes until the skins are charred and wrinkled. Transfer to a bowl, cover with cling film and set aside for 10 minutes or until the skins have loosened and the peppers are cool enough to handle. Using your fingers, peel off and discard the charred skin from the peppers, then deseed and cut the flesh into thick slices.

Meanwhile, if using fresh artichokes, remove the outer leaves and cut the tops off. Trim and peel the stalks. Cut in half lengthways and remove and discard the choke, using a small spoon. Put them immediately in the lemon water to prevent them from discolouring. If you are using preserved artichokes, just drain them thoroughly to get rid of all the oil.

Heat the oil in a medium-sized, heavy-based frying pan over a medium heat and add the thyme, garlic and artichokes. Sauté for 3–4 minutes or until the artichokes are a light golden colour. Add the wine and stir to deglaze, then let it reduce by a third. Season with salt and pepper, reduce the heat to low and simmer, partially covered, for 10 minutes. The artichokes should still be firm at this point; they will finish cooking in the gratin. Remove and discard the thyme and garlic, then add the peppers and put the mixture in a baking dish. Set aside.

To make the goat's cheese sauce, bring the cream to the boil in a small saucepan over a medium heat, then reduce the heat to low and simmer for 10 minutes. Add the goat's cheese and stir until it melts. Season with salt and pepper, then pour the sauce over the artichokes. Place in the preheated oven and bake for 15–18 minutes until the top is pale golden. Serve hot, sprinkled with rosemary.

## *Tarte aux artichauts, oignons et thym*

# ARTICHOKE, ONION & THYME TART

*Preparation time 1 hour, plus making the pastry and chilling*
*Cooking time 50 minutes*

20g/¾oz butter, plus extra for greasing and if using fresh artichokes

1 large garlic clove, peeled

225g/8oz Savoury Short Pastry (see page 23) or ready-made shortcrust pastry

juice of 1 lemon

12 fresh baby artichokes or 225g/8oz drained preserved artichoke hearts

2 tbsp olive oil, plus 1 tbsp if using fresh artichokes

3 eggs

250ml/9fl oz/1 cup double cream

½ tsp freshly grated nutmeg

2 thyme sprigs

3 onions, finely chopped

30g/1oz Parmesan cheese, grated

sea salt and freshly ground black pepper

Grease four individual 12cm/4½in tartlet tins, or one 20cm/8in round tart tin, with butter. Rub with the garlic clove, then reserve the garlic. Divide the pastry into four balls and roll each ball out on a lightly floured surface until it is about 4mm/⅛in thick and 15cm/6in in diameter. (If baking one large tart, roll out the whole quantity of pastry until it is about 4mm/⅛in thick and 25cm/10in in diameter.) Line the tartlet tins with the pastry, taking care not to stretch it. Press down gently to push out any bubbles and roll the rolling pin over the top edge of the tins to trim off the excess pastry. Prick the bases all over with a fork and chill for 25–30 minutes. This will prevent the pastry from shrinking during cooking.

Preheat the oven to 170°C/325°F/gas 3. If you are using fresh artichokes, now is the time to prepare them. First fill a large bowl with water and mix in the lemon juice. Remove the outer leaves from the artichokes and cut the tops off. Trim and peel the stalks. Cut in half lengthways and remove the choke, using a small spoon, and put them immediately in the lemon water to prevent them from discolouring. Heat 2 teaspoons of the oil and about 1 teaspoon of butter in a frying pan over a medium heat. Drain the artichokes, then sauté for 4–5 minutes until golden brown. Remove from the heat and set aside. If using preserved artichokes, just drain them thoroughly to remove as much of the oil as possible. Set aside.

Put the eggs, cream and nutmeg in a bowl and season with salt and pepper, then whisk to combine. Set aside.

Line the pastry case with a piece of baking parchment and fill with baking beans. Bake for 12 minutes. Remove from the oven, discard the beans and parchment and turn the oven up to 180°C/350°F/gas 4.

Meanwhile, heat the remaining butter and oil in a medium frying pan over a medium heat and cook the thyme, reserved garlic and onions gently for 10 minutes, stirring occasionally and making sure that the onions don't brown. Discard the thyme.

To assemble the tart, spread the onion mixture over the pastry case, add the artichokes and then pour in the egg mixture. Bake in the preheated oven for 12–15 minutes (20–25 minutes for a large tart) until light golden and slightly trembling. Sprinkle with the Parmesan cheese, raise the oven temperature to 220°C/425°F/gas 7 and bake for a further 5 minutes to give it some colour. Ideally serve either hot or warm.

This dish takes time but it tastes like heaven. Similar to ratatouille, but baked in layers in a baking dish and finished with Parmesan cheese and rosemary, it becomes a tangy, luxuriant meal. If you can get hold of both green and yellow courgettes and red and yellow peppers, the dish will be beautifully colourful. There are claims that rosemary, besides being powerfully aromatic and delicious, improves the memory and promotes beauty and long life – I'd better get cooking!

*Tian de légumes à la Provençale*

# PROVENÇAL VEGETABLE GRATIN

*Preparation time 20 minutes, plus making the aubergine caviar*
*Cooking time 1 hour 5 minutes*

2 large yellow courgettes, cut into long 5mm/¼in-thick slices

125ml/3fl oz/½ cup olive oil

4 rosemary sprigs

2 large red peppers

1 recipe quantity Aubergine Caviar (see page 41), made with only 4 garlic cloves

sea salt and freshly ground black pepper

freshly grated Parmesan cheese, for sprinkling

**TOMATO BASE**

4 tbsp olive oil

1 onion, chopped

4 garlic cloves, finely chopped

6 tomatoes, chopped

1 tsp thyme leaves

1 tbsp reduced balsamic vinegar

Preheat the oven to 200°C/400°F/gas 6. Combine the courgette slices, oil and rosemary in a bowl and season with salt and pepper, then cover and set aside to marinate.

Meanwhile, put the whole peppers on a baking sheet and roast for 40 minutes until the skins are charred and wrinkled. Transfer to a bowl, cover with cling film and set aside for 10 minutes or until the skins have loosened and the peppers are cool enough to handle. Using your fingers, peel and discard the charred skin from the peppers, then deseed and cut the flesh into long strips.

While the peppers are roasting, make the tomato base. Heat 3 tablespoons of the oil in a medium saucepan over a medium heat. Add the onion and garlic and cook, partially covered, for 4–5 minutes, stirring occasionally, until softened. Add the tomatoes, thyme and the remaining oil, then reduce the heat to low and simmer for 35–40 minutes, stirring often to avoid burning the tomato. If the mixture gets too dry, add a few tablespoons of water. Add the reduced balsamic vinegar and season with salt and pepper.

Heat a ridged griddle pan, or heavy-based frying pan, over a medium heat. Drain the courgettes, giving them a shake to get rid of the excess oil, and reserve the rosemary. Griddle the courgettes for 1 minute on each side or until they have char-grilled marks. This will give them a lovely colour and flavour.

Now you are going to put it all together. Put half the courgette slices in a single layer in a baking dish. Spread half the aubergine caviar over, then cover with half the pepper strips and half the tomato base. Repeat the layers with the remaining ingredients. Chop the rosemary, sprinkle it over the gratin and bake in the preheated oven for 20 minutes. Remove from the oven and turn on the grill to hot. Sprinkle the gratin with Parmesan and flash under the grill for 2–3 minutes until golden brown, then serve.

I hope you've seen the film of the same name, not just because it's very funny but also because it is about a passion for great food that's full of flavour – it shows that its namesake dish can satisfy all tastes, from the discerning gourmet to the lover of good home cooking. The word ratatouille comes from *touiller*, which means 'to stir round or mix', and the recipe originates from Nice in the South of France. For me, this dish not only represents but also encompasses the splendour of the South: full of sunshine, colour and the scent of the Mediterranean.

*Ratatouille à la Provençale*

# RATATOUILLE PROVENÇALE

*Preparation time 20 minutes, plus cooking the rice and pasta*
*Cooking time 2 hours 10 minutes*

100ml/3½fl oz/scant ½ cup olive oil

1 aubergine, peeled and cut into large cubes

1 onion, chopped

4 garlic cloves, crushed

1 red pepper, deseeded and sliced

1 green pepper, deseeded and sliced

1 large courgette or 2 small courgettes, cubed

400g/14oz tomatoes, peeled, deseeded and cut into large cubes

a pinch of caster sugar

1 bouquet garni made with 1 small handful of flat-leaf parsley sprigs and 1 sprig of thyme, tied together with kitchen string

sea salt and freshly ground black pepper (optional)

a small handful of basil leaves, to serve

rice or pasta, to serve

In a large cast iron pan, heat the oil over a medium heat. Add the aubergine and cook for 4–5 minutes until softened but not coloured. Add the onion, garlic and peppers and cook for 2–3 minutes, stirring occasionally, then stir in the courgette, tomatoes and sugar. Add the bouquet garni and simmer gently, partially covered, over a low to medium heat, for 1½–2 hours, stirring occasionally. If, when you take the lid off the ratatouille, it is too wet due to condensation, continue cooking it gently with the lid off, until you get the texture and consistency you want.

When ready, check the seasoning and add some salt and pepper, if necessary. Sprinkle with basil and serve with rice or pasta.

CHEF'S TIP: *A lovely way to use up any leftover ratatouille is to mix it with rice and then stuff tomatoes, which you have deseeded, and bake them in the oven at 180°C/350°F/gas 4 for 25–30 minutes. Or for a quick snack, top pieces of toasted baguette or a rustic loaf, such as pain de campagne, with cold ratatouille. Delicious.*

This is a very special and different risotto, which I normally serve to accompany lamb at The Vineyard – but it tastes wonderful in its own right. Risottos can be done in so many ways: they can be velvety, fragrant, luxurious, elegant or all of these. In this one, the lime brings a refreshing, sharp edge and balances the richness of the cheese and butter beautifully.

*Risotto au citron vert*

# LIME RISOTTO

*Preparation time: 15 minutes, plus making the stock*
*Cooking time: 20 mintues*

135g/4¾oz butter

1 onion, finely chopped

300g/10½oz/1⅓ cup risotto rice, such as arborio or carnaroli

900ml/31fl oz/scant 4 cups Vegetable Stock, plus extra as needed (see page 19)

1½ limes, zest finely grated and fruit peeled and cut into segments, then chopped

90g/3¼oz Parmesan cheese, grated

sca salt and freshly ground black pepper

Heat 80g/2³/4oz of the butter in a medium frying pan over a low heat. Add the onion and cook gently for 3–4 minutes, stirring occasionally, until light golden. Add the rice and turn the heat down to very low. Mix with a wooden spoon until the rice is well coated with the butter and onion.

Add the stock, little by little, stirring continuously until the liquid is absorbed before adding more stock. Carry on adding stock, stirring and then continue to add more stock until the rice has a lovely, creamy texture. Make sure the risotto does not stick to the bottom of the pan.

At the last minute, stir in half the chopped lime segments, the lime zest, Parmesan and the rest of the butter. Place the remaining lime segments, covered, in the fridge to use another day. If the risotto is too thick, add a few more spoonfuls of stock to loosen it up, then season with salt and pepper and serve immediately.

Couscous, made from husked, crushed semolina wheat, is very much a North African dish, however, it has become very popular in France and is now frequently found on brasserie menus. The type of couscous dish you find in France will differ according to the region you are in, what produce is available at the time of year and how spicy you like it. I prefer mine milder and more aromatic than spicy, which is what I have offered here. Also, I like to use the 'moyen', or medium-sized, grain.

## *Couscous de légumes et pois chiches*
# VEGETABLE & CHICKPEA COUSCOUS

*Preparation time 30 minutes, plus making the stock*
*Cooking time 40 minutes*

3 tbsp olive oil

2 courgettes, cut in half lengthways and then into pieces

2 carrots, peeled and sliced

2 turnips, peeled and cut into wedges

1 onion, roughly chopped

1 tsp four-spice mix (including ground ginger, nutmeg, cloves and white pepper)

a pinch each of cayenne pepper, ground coriander and ground cumin

1 tsp coriander seeds

1l/35fl oz/4 cups Vegetable Stock (see page 19)

2 tbsp tomato purée

200g/7oz/generous 1 cup medium-grain couscous

60g/2¼oz butter

125g/4½oz/¾ cup tinned chickpeas, drained and rinsed

sea salt and freshly ground black pepper

a handful of coriander, leaves only, chopped, to serve

Heat 2 tablespoons of the oil in a medium frying pan over a medium heat. Add the courgettes, carrots, turnips and onion and sauté for 5 minutes until the vegetables are pale golden. Stir in the spices, stock and tomato purée and cook over a low heat for 30 minutes, partially covered and stirring occasionally, until the vegetables are tender but still have some bite to them.

When the vegetables have been cooking for about 15 minutes, put the couscous in a heatproof bowl and set aside. In a medium saucepan, put 20g/¾oz of the butter and 250ml/9fl oz/1 cup water, then season with salt and pepper and bring to the boil. Remove from the heat and pour the liquid over the couscous while mixing. Cover the bowl of couscous with cling film and leave to stand for 10 minutes until the couscous is tender. Meanwhile, add the chickpeas to the vegetables to heat through.

Remove the cling film and fluff up the couscous with a fork. Add and stir in the remaining butter, little by little, then season again with salt and pepper. Drizzle the remaining oil over and sprinkle with coriander leaves. Serve the couscous with the vegetables, spooning some of the liquid from the vegetable pan over the top.

Chou braisé

Épinards au beurre et citron

Frisée aux lardons

Haricots verts au beurre et échalottes

Fondant de pommes de terre à l'ail confit

Pommes de terre sautées persillées

Gratin de pommes de terre au vieux comté

## Les Accompagnements et Salades
# SIDE DISHES & SALADS

I always look forward to the change of seasons and how that is reflected on our plates, especially when it comes to side dishes and salads. Each season brings its own special selection of the fresh, the earthy, the tender, the robust and the sweet – something for every mood, every day. Whether steamed, sautéed, roasted, baked or grilled and tossed with olive oil or butter, or served in a salad with a tasty dressing – the possibilities are endless and there is always something delicious and new to enjoy.

*Courgettes à l'huile d'olive et thym*

# COURGETTES WITH OLIVE OIL & THYME

*Preparation time 5 minutes, plus
15 minutes marinating
Cooking time 10 minutes*

4 courgettes, cut into long
  5mm/¼in-thick slices

4 tbsp olive oil

1 tsp thyme leaves

sea salt and freshly ground black
  pepper

Preheat the oven to 180°C/350°F/gas 4. Combine the courgette slices, oil and half the thyme in a small bowl and season with pepper. Set aside to marinate for a good 15 minutes, so the herbs can work their magic.

Heat a griddle pan over a medium to high heat. Spread the courgettes across the lines of the pan and cook for 3 minutes on each side until slightly softened but still retaining some bite. You will need to work in batches, depending on the size of your pan.

Transfer the courgettes to a baking tray, sprinkle with sea salt, a little more pepper and the rest of the thyme leaves and finish in the preheated oven for 3–4 minutes, then serve.

---

*Haricots verts au beurre et échalottes*

# BUTTERED GREEN BEANS WITH SHALLOTS

*Preparation time 10 minutes
Cooking time 10 minutes*

400g/14oz green beans, trimmed

30g/1oz butter

1 shallot, finely chopped

sea salt and freshly ground black
  pepper

Bring a saucean of salted water to the boil and blanch the beans for 4–5 minutes or until al dente, then refresh in a bowl of ice-cold water. Drain and pat dry with kitchen towel.

Heat the butter in a frying pan over a medium heat. Add the green beans and shallot and cook for 2–3 minutes until slightly al dente and well coated with butter. Season with salt and pepper and serve.

## *Chou braisé*

# BRAISED CABBAGE

*Preparation time 5 minutes*
*Cooking time 5 minutes*

1 Savoy cabbage, outer leaves
removed

20g/¾oz butter or 2 tbsp olive oil

⅓ carrot, finely diced

sea salt and freshly ground black
pepper

Cut the cabbage in half, core and slice very thinly. Bring a large saucepan of lightly salted water to the boil and blanch the cabbage for 1–2 minutes, then drain. Rinse under cold water to keep the colour, then pat dry with kitchen towel. Using the same pan you blanched the cabbage in, melt the butter over a low heat. When it is foaming, throw in the cabbage and carrot and cook for 2–3 minutes, stirring occasionally, until tender. Season with salt and pepper and serve.

## *Petits pois à la Française*

# PEAS WITH PAN-FRIED PANCETTA & COS LETTUCE

*Preparation time 10 minutes*
*Cooking time 40 minutes*

30g/1oz butter

12 baby onions, peeled

1 tsp caster sugar

55g/2oz pancetta, cut into
5mm/¼-in thick strips

1 tbsp olive oil

500g/1lb 2oz fresh peas

1 cos lettuce, torn into pieces

sea salt and freshly ground black
pepper

Bring a small saucepan of water to the boil. Melt the butter in another small saucepan over a medium heat. When it is foaming, throw in the onions and cook for 4–5 minutes, stirring occasionally, without browning. Season with salt and pepper, then add enough water to cover and cook for 15 minutes until the onions are soft and the liquid has reduced by half. Add the sugar and cook, stirring, for about 3–4 minutes until glazed, transparent and shiny. Set aside.

Add the pancetta to the boiling water and blanch for 1–2 minutes, then refresh in cold water, drain and pat dry. Heat the oil in a frying pan over a medium heat and sauté the pancetta for 7–8 minutes until crispy and golden brown. Set aside.

Add the peas and cos lettuce to the pan with the onions and simmer, stirring occasionally, for 3–4 minutes. The peas should be tender, the onions still whole and the lettuce just a little crunchy. Add the pancetta and season with salt and pepper. Serve hot.

Walking in the countryside of France, you could be forgiven for thinking that this purple thistle was little more than a weed. But you'd be missing something really special. Catherine de Medici, an Italian princess, recognized this plant for the delicacy it is, and was responsible for bringing it to France in the late 16th century.

*Artichauts violets braisés à la citronnelle, roquette et parmesan*

# BRAISED PURPLE ARTICHOKES WITH LEMONGRASS, ROCKET & PARMESAN

*Preparation time 35 minutes*
*Cooking time 25 minutes*

juice of 1 lemon

16 small purple artichokes or 280g/10oz drained, preserved artichokes

2 tbsp olive oil

4 garlic cloves, crushed with the flat edge of a knife or your hand

2 lemongrass stalks, halved and bruised

1 lemon, halved

150ml/5fl oz/scant ⅔ cup dry white wine

1 small red pepper, peeled if desired, deseeded and chopped

sea salt and freshly ground black pepper

100g/3½oz rocket leaves, to serve

50g/1¾oz Parmesan or a hard cheese such as Comté, shaved, to serve

**DIJON MUSTARD DRESSING**

1 tsp Dijon mustard

2 tbsp olive oil

1 tbsp balsamic vinegar

If using fresh artichokes, fill a large bowl with water and mix in the lemon juice. Remove the outer leaves from the artichokes and cut the tops off. Trim and peel the stalks. Cut in half lengthways and put them immediately in a bowl of water to prevent them from discolouring.

Heat the oil in a heavy-based saucepan over a medium heat. Drain the artichokes and add them to the pan. Cook for 3 minutes, turning occasionally with a wooden spoon, until golden brown all over. Add the garlic and lemongrass and squeeze a few drops of lemon juice over. Cook for a further 5 minutes. If using preserved artichokes, cook for 1 minute before adding the garlic, lemongrass and lemon juice and then for a further 2 minutes.

Add the wine and season lightly with salt and pepper. Cook for 2–3 minutes until slightly reduced, then add the red pepper. Reduce the heat to low and simmer, partially covered, for 10 minutes or until the liquid is reduced by at least half (to about 2–3 tablespoons). The artichokes should be cooked but still quite firm. Remove the artichokes from the pan and set aside for 15 minutes. If there is any remaining cooking liquid in the pan, drain it into a small bowl and discard the lemongrass.

Meanwhile, you can make the dressing. Add the mustard, oil and balsamic vinegar to the cooking liquid. Season with salt and pepper and whisk to combine.

When the artichokes have cooled, scoop out and discard the chokes, using a small spoon. Be careful not to lose any of the artichoke heart just below the choke. Cut the flesh into quarters, if preferred.

Arrange the artichokes on a plate, top with the rocket and Parmesan shavings, sprinkle with the dressing and serve. This is a delicious, refreshing and colourful dish, and also makes a great accompaniment to grilled meat or fish.

The secret with frisée lettuce is to choose one that is really yellow. You need to use all the yellow and only the top section of the light green part. Discard the rest, which can be very bitter. Try keeping the frisée in cold water for 20 minutes before preparing this dish to make it extra firm and crunchy. Delicious with omelette and sautéed potatoes.

## *Frisée aux lardons*
# FRISÉE WITH PANCETTA

*Preparation time 10 minutes*
*Cooking time 15 minutes*

150g/5½oz pancetta, cut into 1cm/½in dice

2 tbsp sunflower oil

1 tsp Dijon mustard

2 tbsp red or white wine vinegar or balsamic vinegar

125ml/4fl oz/½ cup olive oil

1 yellow frisée lettuce, torn into bite-sized pieces

sea salt and freshly ground black pepper

Bring a saucepan of water to the boil and blanch the pancetta for 1–2 minutes, then refresh in cold water, drain and pat dry. Heat the sunflower oil in a frying pan over a medium heat and sauté the pancetta for 8–10 minutes until crispy.

In a small bowl, mix together the the mustard, vinegar and 2 tablespoons water, then whisk in the olive oil until the mixture is quite thick and glossy. Season with salt and pepper.

Put the frisée in a bowl, toss with the vinaigrette and add the crispy pancetta, then serve.

## *Épinards au beurre et citron*
# BUTTERED SPINACH WITH LEMON ZEST

*Preparation time 15 minutes*
*Cooking time 35 minutes*

zest of 1 lemon, cut into thin strips

1 tbsp caster sugar

30g/1oz butter

1 garlic clove, chopped

500g/1lb 2oz large leaf spinach

sea salt and freshly ground black pepper

Bring a small saucepan of water to the boil and blanch the strips of lemon zest for 4–5 minutes to soften and to get rid of any chemicals, then refresh in cold water, drain and blanch and refresh again. Put the sugar in the pan with enough water to just cover and stir to dissolve. Add the zest and simmer gently over a low heat for 20 minutes until glazed. The lemon strips should be candied, shiny and not sticking to each other. Set aside.

Heat the butter in a medium saucepan over a medium heat – it needs to be hot enough for the spinach to wilt quickly, but not so hot that the butter burns! Add the garlic and spinach and cook for 2 minutes until wilted. Season with salt and pepper, then drain and squeeze off any excess liquid.

Serve hot sprinkled with the candied lemon zest.

*Pommes de terre persillées*

# SAUTÉED POTATOES WITH PARSLEY & GARLIC

*Preparation time 10 minutes*
*Cooking time 20 minutes*

400g/14oz new potatoes, cut into
  5mm/¼-in thick slices

2 tbsp sunflower oil

30g/1oz butter

1 small handful flat-leaf parsley,
  roughly chopped

1 garlic clove, chopped

sea salt

Bring a medium saucepan of salted water to the boil and blanch the potatoes for 8 minutes, then drain and pat dry with kitchen towel.

Warm the sunflower oil in a large frying pan over a medium heat. Add the potato slices and cook for 3–4 minutes on each side until golden brown. Just before they are ready, add the butter and let it melt around them – it will give them an extra crispiness and a nutty flavour. At the last minute, throw in the parsley and garlic and sprinkle with salt. Serve immediately.

---

*Ecrasée de pommes de terre à la coriandre et citron vert*

# WARM CRUSHED POTATOES WITH CORIANDER & LIME

*Preparation time 10 minutes*
*Cooking time 15 minutes*

400g/14oz new potatoes

juice and zest of 1 lime

1 small handful of coriander, leaves
  only, roughly chopped

olive oil, for drizzling

sea salt and freshly ground black
  pepper

Bring a large saucepan of salted water to the boil and boil the potatoes for 8–10 minutes until still slightly firm. Drain, refresh under cold water and peel, then crush slightly with a fork – not too much or you will turn them into mash.

Season with salt and pepper, then add the lime juice and zest and the coriander. Drizzle with a little oil and serve.

*Fondant de pommes de terre à l'ail confit*

# FONDANT POTATOES WITH CONFIT OF GARLIC

*Preparation time 15 minutes, plus
making the stock*
*Cooking time 35 minutes*

1 tbsp sunflower oil

100g/3½oz butter, chopped

500g/1lb 2oz small waxy potatoes, such as Charlotte or Jersey Royal, peeled

8 garlic cloves, unpeeled and crushed slightly with the flat edge of a knife or your hand

100ml/3½fl oz/scant ½ cup Vegetable Stock (see page 19) or Chicken Stock (see page 18)

1 rosemary sprig

sea salt and freshly ground black pepper

Preheat the oven to 180°C/350°F/gas 4. Put the oil and butter in a baking dish. Add the potatoes and garlic and bake in the preheated oven for 15–20 minutes or until golden brown all around.

Add the stock and rosemary and bake for a further 15 minutes or until the stock has been absorbed and the potatoes are soft and garlicky. Season with salt and pepper and serve.

---

*Gratin de pommes de terre au vieux comté*

# POTATO GRATIN WITH AGED COMTÉ

*Preparation time 10 minutes*
*Cooking time 50 minutes*

200ml/7fl oz/scant 1 cup full-fat milk

200ml/7fl oz/scant 1 cup double cream

1 tsp freshly ground nutmeg

1 bay leaf

1 garlic clove, cut in half

55g/2oz butter

500g/1lb 2oz floury potatoes, such as Desiree or Maris Piper, thinly sliced

115g/4oz aged Comté cheese or other mature hard cheese, grated

sea salt and freshly ground black pepper

Preheat the oven to 140°C/275°F/gas 1. Put the milk, cream, nutmeg and bay leaf in a medium saucepan over a medium heat and season with salt and pepper. Bring to the boil, then remove from the heat and discard the bay leaf.

Rub a baking dish all around with the garlic clove, then grease it with the butter. Arrange the sliced potatoes in the dish. Stir half the cheese into the milk mixture and pour it over the potatoes. Sprinkle the remaining cheese on top and bake for 45 minutes until melted and lightly coloured.

Preheat the grill to high and grill the gratin for 3–4 minutes or until golden brown. Serve immediately.

*Grosses frites au sel de mer*

# LARGE FRENCH FRIES WITH SEA SALT

*Preparation time 20 minutes, plus*
*1–2 hours chilling*
*Cooking time 45 minutes*

800g/1lb 12oz floury potatoes, such
as Desiree or Maris Piper, peeled
and thickly sliced

1l/35fl oz/4 cups sunflower oil

sea salt

Bring a large saucepan of salted water to the boil. Cut off both ends of the potatoes, peel them and cut them into large, long chips, about 2cm/ 3/4in thick. Wash them to get rid of any excess starch and drop them into the boiling water for about 6–8 minutes. They should still be quite firm when you take them out. Line a tray with kitchen towel, drain the potatoes carefully, so as not to break them, and put them on the tray. Leave to cool, then chill for 1–2 hours.

Heat the oil in a large saucepan over a low heat to 140°C/275°F. If you don't have a thermometer, you can check the temperature by dropping a potato in – if it floats and bubbles, the oil is hot enough. Add the potatoes in 2 or 3 batches, depending on the size of your pan, and fry for 4–6 minutes until firm but with no colour. Remove from the oil with a slotted spoon and set aside to drain on a tray lined with kitchen towel. Repeat with the remaining potatoes.

When ready to serve, increase the temperature of the oil to 185°C/360°F. Fry the chips again in batches for 4–6 minutes until they are a lovely golden colour. Serve hot sprinkled with salt.

*Purée de pommes de terre à la crème*

# CREAMED MASHED POTATOES

*Preparation time 30 minutes*
*Cooking time 55 minutes*

1kg/2lb 4oz floury potatoes, such
as Desiree, Charlotte or Ratte,
unpeeled

100ml/3½fl oz/scant ½ cup full-fat
milk

100ml/3½fl oz/scant ½ cup double
cream

2 garlic cloves, sliced

sea salt and freshly ground black
pepper

Preheat the oven to 200°C/400°F/gas 6. Wash the potatoes thoroughly, put in a large saucepan, cover with water and add a pinch of salt. Bring to the boil, then simmer for 30–40 minutes or until completely cooked through. Drain quickly and place the potatoes on a baking sheet. Put the potatoes in the preheated oven for 10 minutes, then peel.

While still warm, quickly pass the potatoes through a sieve or mouli. Do not allow them to cool, or the mash will be gluey. Cover and set aside.

Put the milk, cream and garlic in a saucepan and bring to the boil. Remove from the heat and pour half the mixture over the potato mixture. Mix well, then add the rest of the liquid little by little. Season with salt and pepper and serve hot.

I find potato salad can be a bit heavy, which is why I love to put plenty of herbs in it. Sorrel and chervil are beautiful herbs but can be tricky to find; market stalls are your best bet. Wild sorrel can be found alongside rivers and in wetlands in the springtime – it looks like an elongated spinach and tastes quite bitter. If you can't find chervil, use extra chives or some tarragon instead. I like to use vinaigrette rather than mayonnaise, because it keeps potato salad light and refreshing. A great one for picnics.

*Salade de pommes de terre nouvelles aux oeufs durs et vinaigrette au Xérès*

# NEW POTATO SALAD WITH HARD-BOILED EGGS & SHERRY VINAIGRETTE

*Preparation time 20 minutes*
*Cooking time 30 minutes*

1kg/2lb 4oz new potatoes

1 fennel bulb, about 5–8cm/ 2–3¼in long

2 eggs

1 tsp vinegar

sherry vinegar, for drizzling

1 small handful of spinach leaves, trimmed

1 small handful of sorrel leaves, trimmed (optional)

1 small handful of mixed lettuce leaves

6 chervil sprigs, finely chopped

2 mint leaves, finely chopped

5 dill sprigs, finely chopped, plus extra to serve

2 spring onions, finely chopped

1 tbsp roughly chopped chives

4 radishes, finely sliced

sea salt and freshly ground black pepper

**SHERRY VINAIGRETTE**

1 tsp Dijon mustard

1 tbsp sherry vinegar

3 tbsp olive oil

Bring a large saucepan of salted water to the boil and simmer the potatoes and fennel stalk over a medium heat for 30 minutes until al dente.

Meanwhile, hard-boil the eggs. Fill a small saucepan with water and bring to the boil. Add the teaspoon of vinegar to the water, as this will make the eggs easier to shell after cooking. Place each egg in a ladle, then slowly and carefully slide the egg into the water so that you don't break the shell. Cook for 8 to 9 minutes, drain and place the eggs under running cold water. When cool enough to handle, shell the eggs, cut in quarters and set aside.

Drain the potatoes and fennel stalk and refresh under cold water. Peel the potatoes, then cut the potatoes and the fennel into thick slices. Put them in a bowl and drizzle with some sherry vinegar.

Arrange the spinach, sorrel and lettuce on a large serving dish, leaving a space in the centre for the potatoes and fennel. Sprinkle the chervil, mint, dill, spring onions and chives over the greens, season with salt and drizzle with more sherry vinegar. Put the potatoes and fennel in the centre of the dish and arrange the eggs around them.

To prepare the vinaigrette, put the mustard, vinegar and oil in a bowl and season with salt and pepper. Whisk to combine, then pour the dressing over the potato salad.

Sprinkle with extra dill sprigs and the radish slices and serve.

# *Les Herbes*

# *Herbs*

I cannot remember a day when there were no herbs in my home or my kitchen, and if such an instance ever were to happen, it would be purely by accident. Would I be able to cook without them? Yes, because I love my trade. Would I like it? Probably not.

It is very hard to explain how essential herbs are to the cooking process or how profoundly they enhance food, whether added to a salad, meat, fish, vegetables or even a dessert. They have such an important place in the kitchen simply because they bring so much taste, so much scent, so much colour to a dish.

If I close my eyes for a few minutes, I can remember what it was like in my childhood when you could smell a wonderful scent of herbs floating around the house when Maman was cooking. It's easy to recall the fragrance of herbs in the freshness of spring or the height of summer, or in your garden, at the market stall or on holiday somewhere such as Provence. There, such vast quantities of so many different herbs grow that the sheer intensity of their scent can be overwhelming and disorienting to the senses. Imagine, if you can, herb fields stretching as far as the eye can see and the sweet scent of thyme mixed with juniper or lavender. What an amazing pleasure, what a delight and what a landscape!

Rather than taking centre stage and overpowering a dish, I think that herbs are best used in the background, as a subtle finishing touch that really completes a dish. The herbs I've selected for use in the recipes in this book are mostly common and easily available, so you can enjoy cooking with them. I have carefully matched them with each recipe for a well-balanced effect.

Like everyone, I have a few favourite herbs that I often use. One of them is thyme, one of the most versatile and commonly used herbs in the kitchen. It is especially good with meats such as pork, lamb and mutton because it aids the digestion of

fats (one reason it is also used as a tisane to revitalize the spirit and refresh the senses), and it's also used in stuffing, ragoût and, of course, the all-essential *bouquet garni* – my standard bouquet garni is made up of a sprig of thyme, a sprig of parsley and a bay leaf.

Another herb I like to use is lavender. Many people do not associate lavender with cooking and are surprised to find it in food, but it is a versatile culinary herb. It is great in meat and poultry dishes as well as desserts. We use it in our specialities at The Vineyard. For example, lavender infused in honey and chilli gives a wonderful flavour to fish dishes. Lavender is everywhere in Provence, with fields full of row after row of purple flowers. The scent invades the whole area – you can smell it in shops, restaurants, cupboards, bathrooms and, of course, in perfumes. It can sometimes be a little overpowering, but, used carefully, the scent and taste of lavender is a pure delight.

Other herbs mentioned in the recipes in this book include parsley, chives, tarragon, chervil, coriander, sage, mint, lemongrass, dill and sorrell. The first four of the herbs I mentioned above are also the main ingredients of *fines herbes*, a staple of French cuisine. They are chopped very finely and usually added right at the end of the cooking process.

Another interesting herb that I recommend you try is *sarriette*, also known as winter savory, which is great in soups, with vegetables or, again, in desserts. Winter savory can be difficult to find in Great Britain, but it is worth tracking it down if you can. For me, it really comes into its own when it is paired with broad beans.

While I'm on the subject of pairings, I should mention there are many complementary relationships between herbs and other ingredients that seem made in heaven – for example, chicken with fresh thyme, duck with lavender, and, of course, lamb with rosemary.

You may be wondering how I could have left off my list so far a herb as important as rosemary, but really, I was simply saving my favourite until last. At home, I rarely cook without rosemary. While it's difficult to explain why I love it so much, I suspect it is partly because it is so evocative of my childhood, reminding me of when I would cut it freshly from our garden at home to go in whatever dish Maman was preparing that day. The smell of rosemary stays on your hand for a while, then, unnoticed, it disappears. But it never leaves you really – instead it stays and wafts around in your memory all your life.

Rosemary has beautiful light purple or white flowers that blossom twice a year. These can be eaten, like many other flowers, including thyme and winter savoury, as well as nasturtiums and pansies, which are often included in salads or used as decoration.

When mixed with other ingredients, rosemary changes character. It is a great herb, but its strength can be lethal, and adding too much of it can make a dish taste bitter. Using rosemary carefully is therefore crucial – but when you succeed, you have a heavenly scent. Make the Tarte Tatin with Rosemary and Toasted Almonds (see page 180) and you will discover how rosemary lifts the apples and mixes with the sugar so well. Or use this versatile herb in a lamb dish, such as Roast Lamb with Mediterranean Vegetables & Sauce Vierge (see page 67) to bring out its many flavours, or skewered in a pineapple to add depth.

Rosemary also has a connection with the great English writer, William Shakespeare, as it is mentioned in several of his plays. Each year on Shakespeare's birthday, branches of rosemary are carried in the streets of Stratford-upon-Avon. What a great day that must be!

Tied with rosemary as a firm favourite is another perhaps less well-known herb – chervil. Again, it is a herb that Maman used a lot, especially in soup. When the soup was almost ready, she would chop the chervil quickly, then just throw it in and serve it. At that point, as the scent of the herb made contact with the heat, the magic began for me, and I'll always remember the way the enticing aroma gradually wafted around and drew me in. I could never resist a second helping, both because of the chervil scent and because the soup was great, too. Chervil has a slightly peppery taste and it goes especially well with buttered carrots, lifting and enhancing the flavour. Unfortunately, chervil can be difficult to find in shops, but you can always ensure a plentiful supply by growing it yourself in spring or summer in your garden or in a pot on the window sill.

In fact, growing a variety of herbs in your very own herb garden, whether in your kitchen or on a balcony, a roof terrace or a window sill, is a great idea, especially if you cook a lot. Not only does this allow you to control the quality of the herbs you use in your cooking (after all, you nurtured those plants yourself), but it also means that you regularly get to use fresh herbs, whose flavour is completely different from and far superior to the flavour of shop-bought dried herbs.

I've expounded at length here and only scratched the surface of the fascinating world of herbs. If you'd like to learn more, I suggest that you begin by following the recipes in this book to get a better idea of how to use them. Then, your understanding of the role herbs play in the kitchen will expand quickly. Once you have a basic knowledge and feel confident enough, start experimenting with using herbs in different ways and with new herbs you discover for yourself. I guarantee you won't regret it.

CLOCKWISE FROM TOP LEFT:
flat-leaf parsley, sorrel, mint,
sage, coriander, rosemary,
chives, chervil, dill

These salads were two of my favourites when I was young, and ones that are very common to find on brasserie display counters. Fresh and easy to serve, they are simple, yet delightfully tasty. If you have freshly picked carrots from your own garden, the second recipe is simply the best – it goes very well with any terrine.

*Salade de concombre à la moutarde de Dijon et ciboulette*

# CUCUMBER SALAD WITH DIJON MUSTARD & CHIVES

*Preparation time 25 minutes, plus 20 minutes resting and making the vinaigrette*

1 cucumber, peeled and cut into 3mm/⅛in-thick slices

1 tbsp French Vinaigrette (see page 20)

1 tbsp double cream

1 tsp Dijon mustard

1 small handful of chives, chopped

sea salt and freshly ground black pepper

Put the cucumber in a large bowl and sprinkle it with salt. Mix well, then set aside for 15–20 minutes to allow the cucumber to release its juices.

Rinse the cucumber quickly under running cold water to remove the excess salt and pat dry with a clean tea towel.

Mix together the vinaigrette, cream and mustard and season with salt and pepper. Pour the dressing over the cucumber, sprinkle with the chives and serve immediately.

*Salade de carottes râpées au cerfeuil*

# GRATED CARROT SALAD WITH CHERVIL

*Preparation time 15 minutes, plus making the vinaigrette*

3 carrots, peeled and coarsely grated

2 tbsp French Vinaigrette (see page 20), or to taste

1 small handful of chervil or coriander, leaves only, chopped

sea salt and ground white pepper

Put the carrots in a large bowl. Stir in the vinaigrette, adjusting the amount you use to taste, season with salt and white pepper and sprinkle with the chervil.

Serve chilled as a starter.

There are lots of different onions, but none as good as the lovely sweet white onions from the South of France, which are for me the perfect partners to bring this tomato salad to life. Here I pair the French white onion with flat-leaf parsley, but you could use red onion and basil instead. Just don't use the large Spanish onion, which has a different flavour, texture and purpose. With a drizzle of freshly cut herbs, olive oil, red wine vinegar, garlic and a touch of salt and pepper, you have the perfect summer salad. Get your baguette ready to dip into those juices and wonderful dressing!

*Salade de tomates aux oignons*

# GARDEN TOMATO & ONION SALAD

*Preparation time 15 minutes*

4 large ripe Italian plum tomatoes or garden round tomatoes, cored and cut into 5mm/¼in-thick slices

8 small yellow tomatoes, halved

4 small round tomatoes, quartered

1 small white onion or 1 large spring onion, white part only, finely sliced

4 tbsp olive oil

2 tbsp red wine vinegar

2 tbsp balsamic vinegar

1 handful of flat-leaf parsley, chopped

1 garlic clove, finely chopped

sea salt and freshly ground black pepper

sliced baguette, to serve (optional)

Arrange the tomatoes on a serving dish and sprinkle the onion over them. Season with salt and pepper and drizzle with the oil and vinegars, then top with the parsley and garlic. Enjoy with sliced baguette, if desired, or as a side dish.

*Tarte au citron et zest de citron vert*

*Mousse au chocolat noir et zest d'orange*

*Clafoutis à la framboise*

*Tarte aux fruits rouges et citron vert*

*Crème au café caramelisée*

*La tarte aux pommes de Maman*

*Crêpes soufflées à l'orange*

## Les Desserts
# DESSERTS

My grandparents' orchard produced so much fruit that Grand-Père had
to think up ingenious ways to store it. I used to pick the fruit (though more
went in my mouth than in my basket), and Grand-Père wove the baskets
himself and filled them with juicy apples, layered with hay. He then stored
them in the attic, and when that was full, he put them in the cellar.
They kept beautifully right through to the spring, enabling us to make
wonderful desserts such as Maman's Apple Tart. The next problem was
where to put the apricots, pears, cherries, redcurrants, blackcurrants …
Apricot Tart and Summer Fruit Tart with Lime are delicious examples
of how we enjoyed them.

Filo pastry parcels are great because you can put almost any fruit you like in them and end up with a fabulous dessert bursting with flavour (just make sure that the fruit isn't too ripe or it will soak the pastry). These little pockets can be as fragrant, as sweet or as spicy as you like: you can add citrus zest, nuts and the spices of your choice. Work quickly and keep the pastry covered with a damp cloth to prevent it from drying out. Served warm and crunchy with a delicate fruit sauce or coulis, they taste like heaven.

*Parcelles de fruits*

# FRUIT PARCELS IN FILO PASTRY

*Preparation time 30 minutes*
*Cooking time 15 minutes*

400g/14oz filo pastry sheets

plain flour, for dusting

100g/3½oz butter, melted

310g/11oz mixed berries or the fruit of your choice, hulled and prepared as necessary

2 vanilla pods, cut in half lengthways

4 petals of 1 star anise

1 tsp freshly crushed black peppercorns

3 tbsp caster sugar

zest of 1 lime

icing sugar, for sprinkling

ice cream or 1 recipe quantity Vanilla Custard (see page 24), to serve

Preheat the oven to 180°C/350°F/gas 4. Unroll the filo pastry, spread it out on a lightly floured work surface and cut it into 16 rectangles, about 30 x 15cm/12 x 6in. Brush each pastry rectangle with some of the melted butter, stacking one on top of the other to create 4 stacks of 4 pastry rectangles. By coating each piece of pastry in butter, you get a beautifully crumbly parcel. It also prevents the pastry from getting soggy when the fruit releases its juices during baking.

Leaving a 3cm/1¼in-wide border along the edges, arrange the fruit on a middle quarter of each pastry stack, keeping the remaining pastry free to fold over. Top each portion of fruit with half a vanilla pod and 1 star anise petal and sprinkle with the black pepper, sugar and lime zest.

Working with one pastry and fruit stack, position it horizontally on the work surface. Brush the edges of the pastry again with some of the remaining butter. Fold the right-hand side of the pastry over the fruit, then fold the left-hand side over to cover the pastry and fruit. Gently pinch the top and bottom open edges together and fold them under the parcel to make sure it is well sealed. Repeat until you have 4 individual parcels.

Transfer the parcels onto a greased baking sheet and sprinkle with icing sugar, which will create a lovely glaze during baking. Bake in the preheated oven for 15 minutes until golden brown and shiny. Serve warm with ice cream or custard.

CHEF'S TIP: *Crumble 1 or 2 amaretti biscuits over the fruit mix in each parcel before folding them up. This adds a subtle almond flavour to the fruit parcels and the biscuit crumbs soak up the fruit juices to help keep the pastry crisp.*

This classic dessert carries the name of the two famous Tatin sisters who invented the recipe. Everybody loves it, I think, because of the smell of warm apple mixed with caramel, and the delicious crunchiness of the light pastry. Just add the contrast of cold crème fraîche or ice cream and you have one of the most fabulous yet simple desserts on the planet. Personally, I like it with a touch of rosemary – when you open the oven door you are enveloped in the incredible perfume of rosemary-scented apples. It is a miracle worth waiting for!

*Tarte tatin au romarin et amandes grillées*

# TARTE TATIN WITH ROSEMARY & TOASTED ALMONDS

*Preparation time 15 minutes, plus chilling*
*Cooking time 1 hour*

220g/7¾oz ready-made puff pastry

plain flour, for dusting

120g/4¼oz/heaped ½ cup caster sugar

40g/1½oz unsalted butter

1 rosemary sprig, leaves only, roughly chopped

3–4 apples such as Cox, Reinette or Golden Delicious, peeled, quartered and cored

a large pinch of toasted flaked almonds, plus extra for sprinkling

crème fraîche, to serve

Roll out the pastry on a lightly floured surface, then cut out a circle slightly bigger than the size of a 20cm/8in flameproof baking or tatin dish. Roll the pastry over the rolling pin and place the pastry on a baking sheet, cover with cling film and chill for 25–30 minutes. This will prevent the pastry from shrinking during cooking.

Preheat the oven to 190°C/375°F/gas 5. Melt the sugar gently in the baking or tatin dish over a medium heat until golden brown, remove from the heat and stir in the butter. Sprinkle about a quarter of the rosemary leaves over. Arrange the apples tightly along the edge of the baking or tatin dish in a circle, then make smaller circles of tightly fitted apples within this circle until the based is covered and all the apples are used. Bake in the preheated oven for 35 minutes.

Remove from the oven, sprinkle the remaining rosemary and toasted flaked almonds over the apples and place the pastry on top, pushing the edges into the dish. Return the tin to the oven and bake for a further 20 minutes until the pastry is golden brown and crisp.

Remove the tart from the oven and leave to cool for a few minutes. Put an upside-down plate the size of the dish on top of the tart and, holding both the plate and dish, flip to unmould onto the plate and sprinkle with extra almonds. Et voilà – a perfect tarte tatin with rosemary. Enjoy while warm. Delicious with crème fraîche.

What used to amaze me about the apples my grandparents grew and stored on the farm was that, even if the skin was as wrinkled as Grand-Père's face, the inside stayed fresh and beautiful – just like him, he used to say! Even after months of storage, the taste was tremendous. So with these apples, my Grand-Mère taught Maman to bake. With these apples, Maman taught me to bake. Whenever I tell my son, Antoine, we are going to visit his Grand-Mère in France, the first question he asks is, 'Can you ask her to bake an apple tart, please, Papa?'

*La tarte aux pommes de Maman*

# MAMAN'S APPLE TART

*Preparation time 30 minutes, plus making the pastry and chilling*
*Cooking time 25 minutes*

1 large egg

100ml/3½fl oz/scant ½ cup double cream

3 heaped tbsp caster sugar

butter, for greasing

1 recipe quantity Grand-Mère's Sweet Pastry (see page 22), Sweet Short Pastry (see page 22), or 225–250g/8–9oz ready-made shortcrust pastry

plain flour, for rolling out the pastry

30g/1oz/scant ⅓ cup ground almonds

4–5 apples such as Cox or Braeburn, peeled, cored and cut into wedges

Mix the egg, cream and sugar in a bowl, beating with an electric mixer or hand-held electric whisk for about 5 minutes until fluffy.

Grease a 24cm/9½in loose-bottomed tart tin with butter. Roll out the pastry on a lightly floured surface until it is about 3–5mm/⅛–¼in thick, then roll the pastry over the rolling pin and place the pastry over the tart tin. With one hand lift the pastry edge and with the other gently tuck the pastry into the bottom and sides of the tin so that it fits tightly. Don't overstretch it or it'll break, and press down gently to push out any bubbles. Trim off any excess pastry by rolling the pin over the top edge of the tin. Prick the pastry base all over with a fork, cover with cling film and chill for 25–30 minutes.

Towards the end of the chilling time, preheat the oven to 180°C/350°F/ gas 4. Place the tart pan on a baking sheet and sprinkle the ground almonds over the tart base, then arrange the apple pieces in a fan shape over the almonds, starting from the outside edge and finishing in the centre. Place the pieces as regularly as you can. Pour the egg mixture over the apples, making sure that the whole surface has been drizzled with the mixture and there are no gaps.

Bake in the preheated oven for 20–25 minutes until pale golden. Remove from the oven and set aside until it has cooled down a little.

Serve the tart while it is still a little warm, when it is most delicious. You don't need cream or ice-cream – it's best on its own with a lovely espresso on the side!

L'Epiphany on 6 January is a big event in France. On that day, we traditionally serve a dessert called la Galette des Rois – a delicious layered feuilleté, or light puff pastry, filled with frangipane almond cream. Another tradition is to hide a coin in the dessert and whoever finds it (without breaking his or her teeth, we hope) gets the crown and is king or queen for the day. The recipe here is a twist on the classic. I use an almond cream that's similar to frangipane, then add apricots and finish it off with toasted almond flakes. It's one of my favourites for texture as well as flavour.

*Tarte à l'abricot*

# APRICOT TART

*Preparation time 30 minutes, plus making the pastry, chilling and cooling*
*Cooking time 45 minutes*

60g/2¼oz/heaped ½ cup ground almonds

60g/2¼oz/¼ cup caster sugar

1 egg, beaten

a few drops of vanilla extract

4 tbsp whipping cream

60g/2¼oz butter, softened, plus extra for greasing

1 recipe quantity Sweet Short Pastry (see page 22) or 225g/8oz ready made shortcrust pastry

plain flour, for dusting

800g/1lb 12oz ripe apricots, halved and stoned

85g/3oz/¼ cup smooth apricot jam

40g/1½oz/½ cup toasted almond flakes

Put the ground almonds, sugar, egg, vanilla extract, cream and half the butter in a bowl and mix until you have a lovely, smooth almond paste, then set aside.

Grease a 24cm/9½in loose-bottomed tart tin with butter. Roll out the pastry on a lightly floured surface until it is about 3–5mm/¹/8–¹/4in thick, then roll the pastry over the rolling pin and place the pastry over the tart tin. With one hand lift the pastry edge and with the other gently tuck the pastry into the bottom and sides of the tin so that it fits tightly. Don't overstretch it or it'll break, and press down gently to push out any bubbles. Trim off any excess pastry by rolling the pin over the top edge of the tin. Prick the pastry base all over with a fork, cover with cling film and chill for 25–30 minutes.

Towards the end of the chilling time, preheat the oven to 180°C/350°F/gas 4. Spread the almond paste over the base of the tart and then arrange the apricot halves on top in a rosace pattern. To do this, arrange the apricots along the edge of the tart so they are slighly overlapping, then make smaller circles of overlapping apricots within this circle until the base is covered and all the apricots are used.

Put the tart in the preheated oven and bake for 30 minutes, then check to see if the apricots are softened, the pastry is pale golden and the almond cream is firm to the touch. If the tart needs more time, bake for a further 5–10 minutes (the apricots will need more time if less ripe). Remove from the oven and set aside to cool for 15 minutes.

Warm the apricot jam in a small saucepan over a low heat, then brush it over the top of the tart. Sprinkle with the toasted almond flakes and serve slightly warm – it makes all the difference.

In Alsace there is a village called Turckheim. It has the charm of many French villages, with its cobbled streets, small shops and a fountain into which so many are anxious to throw their coins. This one stands out in my memory because of the lamplighter, who, every evening at 10 o'clock, strolls the streets in traditional costume, lighting lamps, singing songs and calmly announcing the hour. My father used to go wine tasting there and, as we were still a bit young for it (even by French standards), my mum would take us to a pâtisserie where we could gorge on summer fruit tart with berries so fresh they made our lips and teeth purple.

*Tarte aux fruits rouges et citron vert*

# SUMMER FRUIT TART WITH LIME

*Preparation time 30 minutes, plus making the crème pâtissière , chilling and cooling*
*Cooking time 25 minutes*

1 egg yolk

250g/9oz ready-rolled puff pastry

plain flour, for dusting

reduced balsamic vinegar, for brushing

125ml/4fl oz/½ cup Crème Pâtissière (see page 24) or thick custard

zest of 1 lime

juice of half a lime

55g/2oz/heaped ⅓ cup strawberries, halved and hulled

55g/2oz/scant ½ cup blackberries

55g/2oz/scant ½ cup raspberries

55g/2oz/heaped ⅓ cup blueberries

85g/3oz/scant ¼ cup smooth raspberry jam

Line a baking sheet with baking parchment. In a small bowl, beat the egg yolk with 1 tablespoon water and set aside. Roll out the pastry on a lightly floured surface – the thickness will already be fine, you just need to roll it enough so that you can cut out a 30 x 15cm/12 x 6in rectangle. Reserve the leftover pastry trimmings.

Roll the pastry over the rolling pin and place the pastry on the baking sheet. Brush the edges with the egg yolk mixture, then use the leftover pastry trimmings to make a small border, about 1.5cm/½in wide, around the pastry rectangle. The border will ensure that your Crème Pâtissière and fruit won't run off the sides later. Brush the top of the border with the egg yolk mixture, prick the pastry base all over with a fork, cover with cling film and chill for 25–30 minutes.

Preheat the oven to 180°C/350°F/gas 4. Bake the pastry case for 20 minutes or until light brown, then remove from the oven and transfer to a cooling rack. Brush the base of the pastry with the reduced balsamic vinegar (this helps to make it crispy) and leave to cool. Meanwhile, put the Crème Pâtissière, lime zest and half the lime juice in a bowl and mix well.

Spread the cream mixture over the pastry base and arrange the fruit in lines on top, alternating to create a colourful pattern.

Warm the jam in a small saucepan over a low heat, then brush it over the fruit to glaze. Sprinkle with the remaining lime juice and leave to set in a cool place for 30 minutes, then serve.

*Tarte au citron et zest de citron vert*

# LEMON TART WITH LIME ZEST

*Preparation time 20 minutes, plus*
*making the pastry and chilling*
*Cooking time 1 hour 15 minutes*

250ml/9fl oz/1 cup lemon juice

280g/10oz/1¼ cups caster sugar

zest of 2 limes

7 eggs

250ml/9fl oz/1 cup double cream

butter, for greasing

1 recipe quantity Grand-Mère's
    Sweet Pastry (see page 22), Sweet
    Short Pastry (see page 22), or
    225g/8oz ready-made shortcrust
    pastry

plain flour, for rolling out the pastry

Put the lemon juice and 180g/6¼oz/heaped ¾ cup of the sugar in a small saucepan over a medium heat and cook for 8–10 minutes until reduced. Remove from the heat, add the lime zest and set aside.

Beat the eggs and the remaining sugar in a large bowl, using an electic mixer or a whisk, for about 3–4 minutes until the mixture is fluffy, pale yellow and starting to form ribbon-like shapes when you lift the beaters and it falls back into the bowl. Add the lemon mixture and cream and whisk to combine. Cover with cling film and leave to infuse for 1 hour in a cool place but not the fridge.

Meanwhile, grease a 24cm/9½in loose-bottomed tart tin with butter. Roll out the pastry on a lightly floured surface until it is about 3–5mm/⅛–¼in thick, then roll the pastry over the rolling pin and place the pastry over the tart tin. With one hand lift the pastry edge and with the other gently tuck the pastry into the bottom and sides of the tin so that it fits tightly. Don't overstretch it or it'll break, and press down gently to push out any bubbles. Trim off any excess pastry by rolling the pin over the top edge of the tin. Prick the base all over with a fork and chill for 25–30 minutes. This will prevent it from shrinking during cooking.

Towards the end of the chilling time, preheat the oven to 170°C/325°F/ gas 3. Line the pastry case with a piece of baking parchment and fill with baking beans. Bake in the preheated oven for 15 minutes, then remove from the oven, remove the beans and baking parchment and turn the oven down to 100°C/200°F/gas ½.

Strain the lemon mixture into a medium saucepan and warm it through over a low heat, as gently as possible, stirring continuously. This gives the filling a head start in the oven – a cold filling would have to bake for much longer.

Pour the filling into the pastry case and bake for 40–45 minutes until set. It should tremble slightly when the pastry case is gently shaken before removing from the oven. Leave to cool completely before cutting to serve.

CHEF'S TIP: *If you want to give the tart a twist, sprinkle some icing sugar on top and grill it briefly to give it a brulée effect and add an extra wow factor. This tart needs little adornment, but you could serve with it with raspberries, a coulis or some ice cream.*

# *Les Fromages*
# *Cheeses*

Probably the most widely eaten individual food in the world, cheese is a great source of protein and comes in a stunning variety of names, shapes and packaging. It is one of the most ancient forms of man-made food and references to cheese-making are dotted throughout ancient literature. Even in ancient Sumerian texts dating from 3,000BC, there are references to "twenty soft cheeses".

For me, cheese is an essential part of the dining experience, and no meal is complete without it. In this book, you will find many recipes containing cheese. Almost all of them are French, but Italian Parmesan is also mentioned in some places.

Cheese is very popular in my region of Franche-Comté, which is especially well known for *Comté*, one of the most famous and widely eaten cheeses in France. *Comté* is one of the few products apart from wine to be granted AOC (*Appellation d'Origine Contrôlée*) status, which guarantees the quality and authenticity of the product and protects it from imitation. There are only 42 cheeses, two butters and one cream that are part of this elite. *Comté* is the most popular cheese in France – about 40 per cent of the population consume it, which is an enormous number. Made with cow's milk (45% minimum fat content), it is cooked and pressed. *Comté* is ivory coloured or pale yellow and has a fruity flavour and a strong bouquet. Categorized as a hard cheese and referred to as "cooked", *Comté* is made by heating the milk during production. It is unusual, as the milk has only to reach 40°C/104°F, therefore it is an unpasteurized cheese (lait cru or raw milk) as opposed to pasteurized cheese, which is "cooked" at 72°C/162°F for 20–30 seconds like, for example, *Ossau-Iraty* (see opposite). Maman always prepared a sandwich of *Comté* for us when we came back from school. We absolutely loved the afternoon treat of slices of the cheese in freshly baked baguette.

Every morning, we would have another cheese for breakfast, again with baguette. This time it was *Cancoillotte*, a cheese, interestingly, that is made from another cheese, *metton*, which comes in both factory-produced and hand-made varieties. To make *Cancoillotte*, the *metton* is melted with water or milk, a pinch of salt and a small knob of butter. It's served hot on potatoes or spread cold on bread. I love it, and every time I go to visit Maman, she makes some for us – it is such a delicious treat and it instantly whisks me back to my childhood. *Metton* is made from skimmed milk, which is coagulated, thinly cut and heated to 60°C/140°F, then pressed, pounded and ripened for a few days.

Another cheese from my region is also a big name: *Vacherin Mont d'Or*. It is a seasonal cheese that everyone awaits with great anticipation. Made from the summer milk high in the Massif du Mont d'Or, this cheese is packaged and ripened in a wooden box and bound by a band of spruce bark, which lends it a distinct flavour. After three weeks at a maximum of 16°C/61°F, it is cured on a board of spruce wood and turned, then rubbed with a cloth soaked in brine. The imprint of the cloth gives the cheese a unique appearance.

Before moving on from my region's cheeses, I would like to mention *Morbier*, another outstanding product that is protected by a special AOC label of origin. It is a cow's milk cheese (45% fat content), which is traditionally made by layering the curd obtained from the morning's milk on top of that obtained from the evening's milk, with a protective layer of ash between them. It is best in spring, as it is made with the winter milk production from the chalets of the foothills. It has a firm, creamy interior with a dark line through the middle.

Of course, it is not only my region in France that produces great cheeses, the whole country does. Let me tell you about a few of my favourites. I am a big fan of *Fourme d'Ambert*, a cow's milk blue cheese that comes from the Loire and the Puy de Dôme (45% fat content.) Holding AOC status, it has a firm interior flavoured with parsley, and a dry, dark grey crust mottled with yellow and red. It has a strong flavour and is shaped into a tall cylinder. Another cheese I like very much is *Époisses*, a soft cow's milk cheese named after a village on the Côte d'Or and made in almost every part of Burgundy. It contains 45 per cent fat and has an orange washed crust (done first with sage, then with a Burgundy brandy). At its best in winter, *Époisses* is creamy inside and has a very strong flavour.

My next recommendation is *Livarot*, a full-bodied cow's milk cheese (45–50% fat) from the Calvados region of Normandy. It has a soft, smooth inside and a washed brownish-red rind. Traditionally tinted with annatto (fruit from a tropical flowering tree), this rich cheese is farm-made and also carries an AOC label. The best time to eat it is from November to June. And finally, the last of my favourites – *Fougerus*: a sumptuous cow's milk cheese from the Île-de-France, which has a soft interior and a whitish rind (55% fat content). It is similar to *Brie* but smaller and has fern leaves wrapped around its rind. There is also a variety without the leaves, which is known as *Coulommiers*.

Something happened a few years back, without my noticing. I still don't know why, but I found myself more and more drawn toward pungent sheep's and goat's milk cheeses. As we mature, so does our palate, and perhaps I am now more appreciative of the complexity and strong flavour of these cheeses than I was before. I would like to share some particularly special ones with you. One of my favourite sheep's milk cheeses is *Ossau-Iraty* from the Pyrénées region (50 per cent fat content). It has a creamy, yellow, lightly pressed curd, a smooth orange-yellow rind and a pronounced nutty flavour.

It has AOC status and is great as a snack, on canapés or in a salad. I love *Crottin de Chavignol*, a goat's milk cheese made in the Sancerre region and containing at least 45 per cent butterfat. It has a soft centre and a natural crust mottled with white, blue or brown mould. This cheese can be eaten freshly made, or savoured after it has ripened for three months when it has a more piquant flavour. I also really like *Sainte-Maure de Touraine*, a soft, white goat's milk cheese with AOC status. It is shaped like a log and has a slightly salty, nutty flavour and a distinctive grey, mouldy rind. This cheese contains 45 per cent fat and has a very unusual feature – a piece of straw running through the middle, which leaves a slight dry-hay aftertaste and reminds me of harvest time in late summer. Another of my favourite goat's cheeses is *Pouligny-Saint-Pierre* from the Berry region. It has a smooth curd and a natural rind with a bluish tinge. Made on a farm and awarded an AOC label, it is best from April to November. It is a firm cheese with a strong flavour and, unusually, it is pyramid-shaped.

Nowadays we are very lucky, because in many countries, as in France, more and more fabulous regional cheeses are being crafted by passionate producers on their own small farms. I'm sure you'll agree, we must protect and support them, and recognize their efforts by buying from them directly, or from markets. For me, this is what it is all about – being able to choose and be recommended that special cheese, hand-made traditionally and passed down through generations, not made in a factory where there is no soul, no history, no passion.

The recipes in this book will help you to start on your journey to explore the vast range of cheeses available. But you cannot serve cheese without its best friend – wine. What a match, what a duo, what a great end to a meal! Why not turn them into a great meal on their own by serving them with warm, fresh bread – surely there is nothing better!

LEFT PAGE CLOCKWISE FROM TOP:
Coulommiers, Morbier, Vacherin Mont d'Or, Époisses, Fourme d'Ambert, Pouligny-Saint-Pierre, Crottin de Chavignol

RIGHT PAGE CLOCKWISE FROM TOP:
Fougerus, Livarot, Sainte-Maure de Touraine, Ossau-Iraty, Vieux Parmesan, Vieux Comté

Suzanne was actually my great aunt, but I think her cakes alone were enough to earn her the title of *Grand-Mère!* She always used to say it was the quality of the farm eggs that made them taste so good – the yolks were a deep orange colour – and they gave her cake such lightness and flavour. My father loved going to Grand-Mère's. The first thing he did when he got there was look for the cakes. Grand-Mère liked to hide them so she could tease us that she hadn't made any, but we always knew she had because of the incredible aromas wafting around the kitchen.

## *Le gâteau de Suzanne*
# SUZANNE'S CAKE

*Preparation time 20 minutes*
*Cooking time 40 minutes*

140g/5oz butter, slightly melted, plus extra for greasing

450g/1lb/heaped 3½ cups plain flour, plus extra for dusting

8 eggs

110g/3¾oz/½ cup granulated white sugar

a pinch of salt

250ml/9fl oz/1 cup 2 tbsp crème fraîche

2 tsp baking powder

icing sugar, for dusting

Preheat the oven to 180°C/350°F/gas 4. Grease a 22cm/8½in cake ring with butter and dust it with flour.

In a large bowl, whisk the eggs, sugar and salt together until frothy. Add the crème fraîche and butter and mix with a wooden spoon until it is all incorporated and the mixture is smooth. Add the flour and baking powder and keep mixing until it is smooth again. Pour the mixture into the baking tin and bake in the preheated oven for 40–45 minutes or until cooked. A tip of a sharp knife inserted into the centre should come out hot and dry.

Switch the oven off, open the door slightly and leave the cake inside for a further 8–10 minutes so that it settles without sinking. Remove from the oven and turn out on to a wire rack to cool. To serve, carefully transfer to a serving plate and dust with icing sugar. Simple and delicious!

Originating in the Limousin region, clafoutis soon spread throughout France to become a popular dessert in brasseries all over the country. Traditionally, a clafoutis is made with cherries, but the summer brings an abundance of fruit – tender apricots, juicy plums, fat cherries and wild blackberries, all warm from the sun and begging to be eaten. You can make a delicious clafoutis with any of these, but my favourite is raspberry. The sweetness of the berries and the zing of the lime zest send your taste buds twirling!

## *Clafoutis à la framboise*
# RASPBERRY CLAFOUTIS

*Preparation time 35 minutes*
*Cooking time 25 minutes*

250–280g/9–10oz/2–2¼ cups firm raspberries

zest of 1 lime

125g/4½oz/½ cup caster sugar

50g/2oz butter, half softened and half melted

85g/3oz/⅔ cup plain flour

a pinch of salt

1 egg

1 egg yolk

300ml/10½fl oz/scant 1¼ cups full fat milk

Preheat the oven to 180°C/350°F/gas 4. Put the raspberries, lime zest and 2 tablespoons of the sugar in a bowl. Mix gently, then set aside to macerate for 15 minutes. Meanwhile, grease a 24 x 16 x 6cm/9½ x 6¼ x 2½in baking dish or clafoutis dish (an oval earthenware dish) with the softened butter and sprinkle with another 3 tablespoons of the sugar. Carefully shake the sugar around the dish to make sure it coats the inside.

Sift the flour and salt into a mixing bowl. In a separate bowl, whisk together the egg, egg yolk and remaining sugar, then slowly add the mixture to the flour and mix until incorporated and smooth. Slowly add the milk, stirring until the batter has the consistency of a crêpe batter, then add the melted butter and mix until combined.

Put the raspberries in the clafoutis dish and mix to release the juices. Pour the batter over the raspberries and bake in the preheated oven for 25 minutes until golden brown and set. A tip of a sharp knife inserted into the centre should come out clean and dry. Remove from the oven and serve.

CHEF'S TIP: *It is also fun to make this dessert in individual 150ml/5fl oz/ ⅔ cup ramekin dishes, just reduce the cooking time to 10–12 minutes.*

Sunday evening is a favourite time for making pancakes in our house, and orange soufflé pancakes are a fantastic change to the 'crêpe' served with sugar or jam, and a delicious treat. The soufflé mixture, placed in the top pocket of the folded pancake, is sweet, sharp, light and utterly sublime.

*Crêpes soufflées à l'orange*

# ORANGE SOUFFLÉ PANCAKES

*Preparation time 30 minutes, plus resting and making the custard*
*Cooking time 1 hour*

300ml/10½fl oz/scant 1¼ cup milk

½ vanilla pod

125g/4½oz/1 cup plain flour

2 tbsp vanilla sugar

a pinch of salt

2 eggs

juice and grated zest of ½ orange

1 tbsp orange liqueur, such as Cointreau or Mandarin Imperial

40g/1½oz butter, melted, plus extra for frying, if needed

icing sugar, to serve

**ORANGE SOUFFLÉ MIX**

4 egg whites, beaten

40g/1½oz/scant ¼ cup caster sugar

2 tbsp Vanilla Custard (see page 24)

juice and grated zest of ½ orange

In a small saucepan, warm the milk over a low heat for 2–3 minutes. Cut the vanilla pod in half and scrape the seeds into the warmed milk, add the pieces of pod and leave to infuse for 30 minutes. Discard the vanilla pods.

Put the flour, vanilla sugar, salt, eggs, orange juice and zest, and liqueur in a bowl. Add one-third of the milk mixture and the melted butter and whisk until smooth. Alternatively, just pop it all into a blender if that's easier for you and blend for 2–3 minutes. Slowly whisk or blend in the remaining milk. Make sure that there are no lumps in the batter and that the consistency is quite runny so your pancakes will be thin and light. If you do it gradually like this, you won't have to let the batter rest.

Heat a non-stick pancake pan or a 15–18cm/6–7in-wide non-stick frying pan over a medium to high heat. (Using a non-stick pan means you won't have to add butter before cooking the pancakes, as you already have some in the batter, though of course it can make flipping the pancakes easier if you do.) Using a ladle, put enough batter in the pan to thinly cover the base, tilting the pan, if necessary. Cook for 1–1½ minutes. Then comes the fun part – try to flip it. Use a spatula if you want to stay on the safe side. Cook for a further 1–2 minutes on the other side, then transfer to a plate and set aside at room temperature. You should be able to make about 12–15 pancakes.

Preheat the oven to 200°C/400°F/gas 6. To make the soufflé mix, put the egg whites and sugar in a bowl and beat with an electric mixer for 8–10 minutes (or whisk by hand) until firm. Put the custard in another bowl and whisk in half the egg white mixture to make a smooth paste, then fold in the remaining egg white mixture. It should be silky but firm.

Fold each pancake in half, then in half again. Put them in a non-stick baking tray, making sure they're not too close together so they have room to grow. Lift the top layer of each pancake and spoon the soufflé mix into it. Bake in the preheated oven for 8–10 minutes until the pancakes rise like a soufflé but stay firm. Remove from the oven, dust with icing sugar and serve immediately. Once you start eating these, you'll never want to stop!

Luxurious, smooth crème caramels – make them in the morning and they'll be set and ready in time for dinner. It's worth it just to see the look on your guests' faces when you appear with a blowtorch to finish them off (the crème caramels, not the guests!). I've made them here with coffee, but you can substitute the coffee with many other flavourings and spices, such as vanilla, cinnamon, chocolate, lemongrass and star anise.

## *Crème au café caramelisée*
# COFFEE CRÈME CARAMEL

*Preparation time 15 minutes, plus*
*4 hours chilling*
*Cooking time 1 hour*

175g/6oz/heaped ¾ cup caster sugar

250ml/9fl oz/1 cup milk

100ml/3½fl oz/scant ½ cup double cream

15g/½oz/¼ cup instant coffee granules

3 eggs

2 egg yolks

40g/1½oz soft brown sugar, to caramelize (optional)

Have ready four 150ml/5fl oz/²/₃ cup ovenproof pots (or six 100ml/3½fl oz/½ cup pots if you want to serve smaller portions). Put 100g/3½oz/scant ½ cup of the caster sugar in a small heavy-based saucepan and melt over a medium heat, stirring with a wooden spoon until it melts and turns a pale caramel colour. Immediately pour it into the pots and swirl them around to coat the base and sides with the hot caramel. Use a tea towel to protect your hands. Leave to cool completely.

Preheat the oven to 110°C/225°F/gas ½ and line a deep baking dish with greaseproof paper. The paper will direct the bubbles away from the pots, providing a more gentle cooking process so the custard doesn't curdle. Combine the milk, cream, coffee granules and 50g/1¾oz/scant ¼ cup of the caster sugar in a saucepan and gently bring to the boil over a low heat, stirring to dissolve the sugar and coffee. In another bowl, whisk together the eggs, egg yolks and remaining caster sugar for 1–2 minutes until pale and the sugar has dissolved. Pour the boiling milk mixture into the egg mixture, whisking as you go.

Divide the mixture into the pots and put them in the baking dish, then pour enough warm water into the dish to come half way up the sides of the pots (this is called a bain-marie). Put the bain-marie in the preheated oven and bake for 45 minutes or until the tip of a sharp knife inserted into the centre of a pot comes out clean. If necessary, return to the oven and cook for a further 5–10 minutes. Remove from the oven and transfer the pots to a wire rack to cool completely. Cover with cling film, then refrigerate for a minimum of 4 hours.

I like to caramelize the creams before serving. If you want to do this, you will need a bit of courage and a blowtorch! Sprinkle the tops of the pots with the brown sugar and caramelize with the blowtorch for a few seconds. If you haven't got a blowtorch, you can pop them under a hot grill for about 1 minute.

Everyone needs a little chocolate in their life, or so my wife Claire tells me. The combination of chocolate and orange is one of my son's favourites, too, so this dessert never lasts long in our house. You'll need a good-quality chocolate for this: I recommend 66%–70% pure cocoa, which has a slight bitterness and a hint of spice. One thing, though, watch out for the chocolate disappearing: it seems to evaporate in our house whenever my back is turned!

*Mousse au chocolat noir et zest d'orange*

# BITTER CHOCOLATE MOUSSE WITH ORANGE ZEST

*Preparation time 20 minutes, plus
  1 hour chilling
Cooking time 20 minutes*

1 orange

90g/3¼oz/heaped ⅓ cup caster
  sugar

100g/3½oz plain chocolate
  (66–70% cocoa solids), chopped
  into small pieces

3 egg yolks

150ml/5fl oz/scant ⅔ cup double
  cream

1 tbsp icing sugar

Pare the zest from the orange into fine strips using a zester or a small, sharp knife, cutting any pith away. Put the zest in a small saucepan, cover with cold water and bring to the boil over a medium heat. As soon as it starts to boil, remove from the heat. Refresh under cold water, drain and repeat this entire process once more.

Using the same pan, return the zest to the pan and add 2 tablespoons of the caster sugar and 3 tablespoons water, stirring to dissolve. Bring to the boil and cook for 4–5 minutes, or until the zest becomes transparent, then leave the zest strips to cool in the syrup. When cold, drain and set aside.

To make the chocolate mousse, put 75g/2½oz of the chocolate in a heatproof bowl and rest it over a saucepan of gently simmering water, making sure the bottom of the bowl does not touch the water. Heat for 4–5 minutes, stirring occasionally, until the chocolate has melted, then remove from the heat and keep warm. In a separate heatproof bowl, mix together the remaining sugar, egg yolks and 2 tablespoons warm water. Rest the bowl over the saucepan of gently simmering water, making sure the bottom of the bowl does not touch the water. Beat the mixture for 8–10 minutes until it turns pale, thickens and forms ribbon-like shapes when you lift the whisk and the mixture falls back into the bowl. Slowly stir in the melted chocolate until well combined.

In another bowl, whip the cream and icing sugar until soft to medium peaks form, then gently fold it into the chocolate and egg mixture until you obtain a lovely, smooth mixture, taking care not to overwork it. Divide the mousse into four glasses, glass dishes or large ramekins. Cover with cling film and chill for 1 hour before serving. If chilled for longer, remove from the fridge 30 minutes before serving.

Just before serving, melt the remaining chocolate in a heatproof bowl over simmering water. Swirl the chocolate over each mousse, then top with the orange zest and serve.

This is one of my favourite desserts – I just love the intriguing contrast between the cold, creamy custard and the brittle, hot layer of caramelized sugar. For me, crème brûlée is particularly delicious served with a fruit purée – raspberry and blackberry are both sensational. They bring the perfect acidity needed to balance the richness – just as you're being lulled into luxury by the sugar and cream, a sharp burst of summer fruit explodes in your mouth. It's a wonderfully decadent treat.

*Crème brûlée à la purée de framboises*

# CRÈME BRÛLÉE WITH RASPBERRY PURÉE

*Preparation time 30 minutes*
*Cooking time 50 minutes*

4 egg yolks

80g/2¾oz/⅓ cup caster sugar

270ml/9½fl oz/1 cup double cream

25g/1oz/2 tbsp soft brown sugar, for sprinkling

**RASPBERRY PURÉE**

100g/3½oz/scant 1 cup raspberries

grated zest of 1 lime

2 tbsp caster sugar

First make the raspberry purée. Put the raspberries, lime zest and sugar in a bowl and mix gently using a fork. Set aside to macerate for about 15 minutes, then crush the mixture into a purée, using a fork. There's no need to pass it through a sieve as you want to keep the seeds to give the purée more flavour.

Preheat the oven to 150°C/300°F/gas 2 and line a deep baking dish with greaseproof paper. The paper will direct the bubbles away from the pots, providing a more gentle cooking process so the custard doesn't curdle. Whisk the egg yolks and caster sugar together in a heatproof bowl until smooth. Gently heat the cream in a saucepan over a low heat, then slowly pour it into the egg yolks, whisking as you go. Make sure it is smooth with no lumps, otherwise you'll end up with scrambled egg.

Divide the purée equally into four 150ml/5fl oz/⅔ cup ramekins, then divide the egg and sugar mixture equally into the ramekins and put them in the deep baking dish. Pour enough warm water into the tray to come halfway up the sides of the ramekins (this is called a bain-marie) and place the bain-marie in the preheated oven. Bake the brûlées for 35–40 minutes until set but still slightly trembling when shaken, then remove from the oven and transfer the ramekins to a wire rack to cool until set.

Preheat the grill to high. Sprinkle the brûlées with the brown sugar and put them on a baking sheet. Grill for 2–3 minutes until the sugar is caramelized. Serve immediately.

# INDEX

# AUTHOR ACKNOWLEDGEMENTS

I would like to thank the following people:
My family, for all their support and friendship; my suppliers: Eric Charriaux at Premier Cheese, Martin at Channel Fisheries, the Bread Factory and John Piper at Oakleaf Ltd.; Jane and her team, for providing me with a Thermomix, to help with some of the recipes – it's a great tool; The Vineyard management, my head chef, Frédéric, and my team for allowing me time out to do the book and photoshoot; my agent, Rosemary Melbourne, for her support; the team at the HHB Agency, especially Heather Holden-Brown for her constant support and cheerful nature, and for putting up with me; my publishers: Duncan, Grace, Manisha, Camilla and the rest of the gang for their enormous patience, for having faith in me and for their guidance to see the project through; the photographer Yuki, for her wonderful talent, her sense of humour and for keeping me on track; Aya, my assistant, who's a great cook and lots of fun, and who bosses me around (with good reason!) – it's super to work with her; Heston Blumenthal for his foreword, his friendship and for always being such a gentleman; James Martin for sending me such a lovely note and for being my friend; my dad, Daniel Senior, for passing on to me all his passion and respect for nature; and finally two very special people: my son Antoine, for being who he is – beautiful, funny, and loving life and food; and my wife Claire, for being there throughout the project and helping me to translate from my "franglais" into lovely, readable text. Without her, her patience, her friendship and her Italian charm, it would have been a much bigger challenge.